ALSO BY SUSAN POWTER

Stop the Insanity!
The Pocket Powter
Food

by

SUSAN POWTER

C'mon America, Let's Eat!

SUSAN'S FAVORITE LOW-FAT RECIPES TO FIT YOUR LIFESTYLE

A FIRESIDE BOOK

PUBLISHED BY SIMON & SCHUSTER

New York London Toronto Sydney Tokyo Singapore

FIRESIDE
Rockefeller Center
1230 Avenue of the Americas
New York, NY 10020

Designed by Karolina Harris
Illustrations by Sally Mara Sturman
Interior photographs by Cynthia Stern; food styling by Helga Weinrib Rudtke
and Deborah Mintcheff; prop styling by Linda Engelhardt

Manufactured in the United States of America

1   3   5   7   9   10   8   6   4   2

Library of Congress Cataloging-in-Publication Data
Powter, Susan.
C'mon America, let's eat! : Susan Powter's favorite low-fat
recipes to fit your lifestyle.
p.   cm.
1. Cookery, American.   2. Low-fat diet—Recipes.   I. Title.
TX715.P889   1996
641.5′638—dc20   95-44765
CIP
ISBN 0-684-81317-3

Acknowledgments

This book couldn't have been written without the hard work and dedication of my coworker and friend Suzi Kressler. Who woulda thunk it, Suzi—a conversation by the toddler pool years ago leading to all this! I look forward to all the joy and the pain of the next however-many stages. You make me think and feel, which helps me grow. Thank you.

To my sons—for understanding when our Sunday mornings together turned into a workday for Mom, so that every woman who wants more information to change the way she looks and feels gets it.

Bob and Sarah—from Cybersex to correct punctuation, OH what fun our conversations are. . . . Here's to the next fifty books together.

Trudy—your food is the best. Thank you.

To the taste-testing women in beauty parlors and kitchens all over this country who told us exactly what they thought. I've always said it and you've proven it to be true: "If you want to know, just ask the women of America."

This book is dedicated to the women I meet everywhere I go who make it very clear to me that we do care about our health. We are making better choices for ourselves and our families. We are willing to work for it, and it's about a lot more than losing weight—it is and always has been about regaining control of our lives and looking and feeling the way we want to look and feel.

The smile in your eyes. The warmth of your hug. The laughter we share when we talk about the insanity that affects all of our lives lets me know that we are stopping it. Enjoy—this book's for you.

Contents

Entrees

Vegetables

Rice and Beans, Breads and Grains

Pasta and Pizza

Sauces, Dips, and Spreads

Desserts

Introduction

There's a big celebration going on, and I need your help. We're talking party. Big, big bang of a festival. This firework-able splash isn't happening outside by the pool, next to the barbecue grill, or in any ballpark you've ever visited, and you won't find anybody there in formals or costumes.

This celebration takes place right here in the pages of this book.

Do you wanna know what we're celebrating and what the heck any of it has to do with you, food, cooking, and me wearing a fifties waitress outfit on the cover??????

Not to worry, my friends. I have the answers for ya: AMERICA.

Celebrating America, that's what we're doing.

Celebrating America by highlighting, featuring, starring American food. It's a damn good way to get you some great information that's gonna make your life a whole lot easier and your thighs a whole lot thinner. You get to come to a celebration within a celebration, my own little party.

Not making an ounce of sense? Don't worry, it will.

Why am I celebrating? Sure, things have been going well over the last couple of years (a few problems here and there, but nothing to complain about), but that's not the reason for the party in a book.

Am I celebrating because I'm just in the mood to celebrate? NOOOOOOOOO.

Here's a hint:

America is the star of this book . . .

The national anthem keeps playing with every word typed . . .

There's a courtroom involved. (My lawyers are rubbing their hands together now. Back down, boys and girls! This doesn't involve you.) . . .

There's a small test involved of which AMERICAN history is the focus . . .

A point behind the American motif . . .

A connection between apple pie and me . . .

YOU GUESSED IT: I AM SHOOTING FOR CITIZENSHIP.

Come on, MY FELLOW AMERICANS, let me in. I'm trying to become one of you. I thought one of the best ways to do that was to write a tribute to American food, as an almost American citizen . . . because I really want to be one.

I, Susan Powter, born and raised for the first ten years of my life in Australia, lived for the next twenty-six years of my life as an Australian citizen in America, want to legitimize myself. And the first thought of every new American citizen is a cookbook, of course.

I'd like to invite the whole country to my almost citizenship celebration. We'll make it useful. You'll get some of the best low-fat recipes you've ever tasted. And while we're at it, let's talk about a couple of things that really need some talking about when it comes to America and our food.

I have to talk low fat because that's my deal. Used to be 260 pounds. Minus 133 pounds. From very unfit and overfat to very fit and lean . . .

Short white hair.

Fitness terrorist.

Stop the Insanity.

Any of this ringing a bell . . . THE LIBERTY BELL, THAT IS?

That's me, Susan Powter. Low fat and leaner, very important. Looking and feeling the way you want to look and feel, very important. Shrinking your body, getting the thighs of your dreams, we're gonna get that, we know. But there are a few other little problems that need a wee bit of discussion.

Let's call them the potential party crashers!

The unwelcome relatives!

The social slobs that didn't RSVP but showed up anyway!

And one of these unwelcome little buggers is hitting us right in the heart (literally) of our celebration.

You see, when you're talking American food, you have to consider things such as . . .

Disease. I know, I know, it's not anything you want hanging around your celebration, but truth be known, we (don't you love that you and me are almost we—as Americans, not that we're married?) are second in the world in heart disease, a disease directly connected to what we are putting into our mouths.

Obesity. An epidemic in this wonderful country of ours.

Excuse me, I'm having a close-to-citizenship moment. "OF OURS." DID YOU HEAR THAT? OURS.

OH, SAY CAN YOU SEE
By the dawn's early light
What so proudly [proudly being the big word, because I would be] we hailed . . .

Pardon. Back to the point.

Our being fat—is it connected to the amount of fat we are taking in daily? I think it is! All you gotta do to get the definite on that one is ask yourself: Is your body manufacturing however much extra fat that's all over your body? Is it

19

just appearing out of thin (sorry!) air? You walk around and the stuff sticks to you like glue?

No. Sorry. It's coming from somewhere, and your best guess would be *the end of your fork.*

Absolutely a bit of a bummer when you think of the stats and the reputation that's connected to the American diet. Take it from me: I just got back from Europe, and I didn't hear the end of it:

"You are all so fat"—the French.

"Americans are gluttons"—the Italians.

"You are all dying of disease"—the English.

"You have no idea what good food is. All you know is processed, canned, and instant."

"You . . ."

"You . . ."

"You . . ."

ENOUGH!

My response (on French national TV, thank you very much):

"Sure, we've got a bit of cleaning up to do when it comes to what we are putting into our mouths. We know that, and we're working on it. But let me tell you something, Pépé Lepew. (I was talking to a self-righteous male French doctor, and, true, the Pépé Lepew part didn't go over too well. But, hey, I was defending us, and what people do on the front lines is a matter of survival—right, veterans?) You may not be dropping like flies because of heart disease, but you are dying left, right, and center of lung cancer because I've never seen smoking like I've seen in the last few days. Self-inflicted disease is self-inflicted disease no matter how you look at it. Heart disease is a cardio issue, and so is not being able to breathe. Lung cancer ranks right up there with the old respiratory issues. So, Mr. Self-Righteous, what do you think of that?"

Sure I defended my soon-to-be country—and defended it well, I might add—but you know what? Between you, me, and every other American on the planet, we aren't doing very well. We have lost a bit of national pride in the food department, and, damn it, it's time we got it back.

American food is fabulous. The old favorites have to be defatted a bit, granted, but, hey, should we be ashamed of our burgers and dogs?

Hell, no!

Give up the barbecue?

Hell, no!

But we also shouldn't be willing to fall right into the killer, high-fat, greasy food categories of the world.

Hell, no.

Come on, say it again . . .

HELL, NO!

Let's get back some of the old Barbecuing, Ballpark, Thanksgiving, Family Picnic Pride. All we have to do is reach down to the bootstraps of the old American ingenuity!

Let's lighten it up a little—not in taste, just in the amount of fat that's running through (or not through) our arteries and suffocating our bodies.

Ask not what your country can do for you, ask what you can do for your country's food . . .

I have a dream, a whipped cream dream . . .

I regret that I have but one burger to give for my country . . .

Fourscore and seven desserts ago . . .

It's time and it's here. More reasons than you can shake a stick at (whatever the heck that means) to write a cookbook, but the buck doesn't stop at the front door of my citizenship suck-up/cookbook.

There's one more reason why I wrote this book.

The most important reason.

You.

You can't get enough—low-fat ideas, that is.

Let me guess: Running low on ideas when it comes to feeding the family?

Just don't know anymore what to do with that meat-and-potatoes guy? (Other than what to feed him, I can't help you.)

Who can get enough food information? There are always meals to plan, kids to feed, and food to think about, and just when you thought you had this high-volume, low-fat thing down, you find yourself getting bored out of your skull.

Sick of potatoes everything!!

Don't even want to think about beans and . . .

Forget about grains—who cares?

Is your life anything like mine? Most nights you're crawling in the door after a long, long day, and you're supposed to get low-fat creative? Forget about it. Isn't "healthy anything" the last thing on your mind when you've just walked in the door at 7 P.M. and there's still laundry, the kids' homework, and the house to contend with?

The fact that most of the time you just say to hell with it and reach for the closest, easiest, highest-fat food means you're just like the rest of us. I'm telling you the truth when I say that all of us fail miserably when it comes to making "perfect for your body" and the "highest-quality" life choices when we're tired, fed up, and hungry.

You shouldn't have to turn into the Julia Child of the low-fat nineties every night at dinner . . .

There's no reason for you to rack your brain for a low-fat version of the family's favorite meal . . .

Enough with having to know all there is to know about cholesterol and saturated fat when all you want to do is get everyone fed and go to bed . . .

And besides, you don't have to anymore, because it's here: the "splatter the food, bend the pages, photocopy and give to your best friend" kind of cookbook.

It's yours.

It's understandable.

And it's easy to apply to you and your family's life.

And the bonus . . .

One of the most important parts . . . Low, low, low fat.

If it's dress sizes you want to drop and a lower-fat lifestyle you're interested in, then you're in the right place wherever you are reading this book.

The motto of this book: It's gotta be great tasting. It's gotta work for the whole family. It's gotta be quick and easy.

Here's a thought. Spend your cash on a cookbook that has food the family will actually eat.

Rosemary chicken with parsley sprigs—what's up with that? Who's gonna make that for the family dinner?

Let's blow the social pressure of having to do it "right" or "pretty" right out of the water.

I've read it. Seen the fixer-uppers in *Better Houses and Porches*. Yeah, my living room looks the same way theirs does when I've tried to staple the upholstery on . . .

You don't think I've tried to paint my own T-shirts? If it's Christmas trees on T-shirts you want I've done them, and nobody would be caught dead in mine.

I've read the cookbooks. Who hasn't? I mean, Betty Crocker. Love her. She's top billing when it comes to cookbooks, there's no doubt about that. The Grand Dame of the Kitchen. The Royalty of Roasts. Someone we all aspired to be.

But just between you and me, was she real? Has anyone ever met Bet? Has a photo ever been published? Do we know this woman that all America has loved for years?

You see, we've all bought the books, read the recipes, and tried to do the creative thing, but we all seem to be facing the same "I just can't do it well," "I just can't get it together," "I just can't be creative enough" feelings when it comes to feeding ourselves or our family in the low-fat nineties. It never seems to come out the way Betty made it, and you end up feeling like the entertainment and culinary loser of all time.

Well, it's over. You're not gonna feel like a horse's ass (tied to a post in front of a saloon, drinking whiskey, and checking out the dancing girls of the Old West—those were the good old days?) anymore.

With the women of this country working in the home, out-side of the home, around the home—building the home—it's time that old Betty (yes, let's admit that Betty Crocker has gotta be 108 by now and is no longer in the kitchen slinging the hash browns) hands the crown over.

Face it, Betty: Times have changed, and we need help.

Who in the nineties isn't sitting at the kitchen table, totally confused, clueless, and in need of a little help?

The food pyramid changes every day, doesn't it? What's important now? Meat, milk, grains, fruit? How much of any of it are we supposed to have so that we won't shrivel up and die or explode from obesity and heart disease? Your neighborhood doctor (doesn't exist, but for the sake of nostal-gia let's pretend that he/she—had to slip "she" in—does) is coming out of the closet and saying, *"Oooops,* what we meant to tell you is that meat and milk are loaded with saturated fat and cholesterol and are the biggies in the contribution of heart disease, strokes, cancer . . . " and on and on it goes.

Don't you just want your questions answered and dinner on the table?

Ladies, ladies, ladies, don't you think it's time to join forces and tell it like it is???? We are confused. We are guilty. We feel as if we are incapable anymore of putting a meal together that doesn't make us look politically, socially, and morally inadequate. Don't you just want to lose weight and keep it off?

Isn't it about making your life a little simpler and looking and feeling the way you want to look and feel?

So . . . let's get on with it.

It's time for a bit of a change, and this year *will* be different because this is the Year of the Ending of Confusion—a Susan Powter addition to Chinese calendars: Year of the Pig, Year of the Dog, Year of the Ending of Confusion . . . don't you like the sound of it?

We are going to eat and enjoy our food. We're going to get back to the good old-fashioned favorites: scream the national anthem, draped in reds, whites, and blues; feed the friends and family; go to potluck dinners with a renewed sense of pride; entertain again; not avoid the holidays like the plague; *and* get leaner. It's the basic "Let's just cook a good meal that tastes great but is not going to make us fat and unhealthy" way of thinking that I live with every day, and it works.

Is that what you want?

Have you been looking everywhere? Can't figure out why someone just doesn't give you what you need?

OK, OK, OK—

Twist my arm!

It's done.

COME ON AMERICA, LET'S EAT!!!!

Soups have saved my butt thousands of times. A good soup in the fridge is worth a whole lot when you're running late and forget that there is a household of hungry people waiting for you.

This diversified food category works just as well for one. I have a friend who's single, no kids, and a soup a week is her way of making sure she eats—poor thing, she's got nothing to think about but herself and can't seem to pull it together to think food. Must eat something to live . . . a bowl of soup and salad, bowl of soup and bread, bowl of soup and rice, bowl of soup and cereal (you know how those young single people are, not that I remember not having to think about dinner for three or four, and not that I want to). Make a bunch of great soups, put them in your fridge, and eat them all week; it's one less thing for you to have to think about.

Soups

Corn and Potato Chowder

Corn: Otherwise known to American Indians as maize. (I know that from those margarine commercials which I'm sure anyone of Indian heritage hates with a passion.)

And *potato:* Idaho, right? Home of the Spud boys? Put them together, and you've got yourself a soothing, light, satisfying, get-you-over-the-hungry-hump, fabulous late-night bowl of Great Basic Soup that can be casual . . . Or black tie.

Fancy Schmancy

Corn and Potato Chowder with . . . Garlic Herb Bread (see page 212) and garden salad.

Makes you feel very European. Impresses the heck out of family and friends, and you don't have to be Martha Stewart to pull it off. Believe me, I did it, and I'm the woman who can't even paint a Christmas T-shirt. This little number does wonders for your entertainment self-esteem.

Leftovers

This soup reeks American because it's a leftover dream. Put it in the fridge. Two days later, pull it out and serve it with grilled cheese and fresh veggies. We're talking great lunch, ten minutes to make, and simple, simple, simple.

Fab Ideas

Add crumbled turkey bacon, salsa, nonfat sour cream, croutons, nonfat cheddar cheese.

Olive oil spray
½ cup chopped onion
½ cup chopped red bell pepper
3 cups frozen corn, thawed
3 cups vegetable broth
⅛ tsp cayenne pepper
2 medium potatoes, peeled, cubed, and cooked till tender
2 tbsp chopped parsley
1 tbsp chopped green onion

Sauté the onion and red pepper in a pot lightly sprayed with oil until the onions are very limp.

Put 2 cups of the corn and 1 cup of the broth in a blender and process until smooth.

Add the puree to the pot of onions and peppers.

Add the cayenne pepper, potatoes, and remaining corn and broth.

Heat through, sprinkle parsley and green onion on top, and serve.

Nutritional:

Serving Size 9¹/₂ ounces
Servings per Recipe 6
Calories 117
Total Fat 0.272 gram
Saturated Fat 0.03 gram

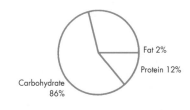

Fat 2%
Protein 12%
Carbohydrate 86%

Cream of Potato Soup

Cream without fat? Real, thick, white, creamy flavor that doesn't taste like skim milk potato soup? Don't ever let 'em tell you that you can't eat something tasty that's low-fat. If they do, throw 'em a bowl of this Cream of Potato Soup.

$\mathcal{F}$ab Ideas

This is so thick and creamy that it can easily be a main course with a salad and some fab dinner rolls.

Or you can always maintain the tradition of the fancy soup before the meal with this.

Be as fancy schmancy as it gets just by adding two chopped sautéed leeks (white part only) and, bingo, you've got vichyssoise.

We should change the name of this soup to Versatile Cream of Potato Soup because if you add one cup of chopped spinach (squeeze the juice out of the spinach first) and blend with a squeeze of lemon, you've got cream of spinach soup.

Last but not least, on the most versatile soup on the planet, your Cream of Potato Soup is a perfect base for other vegetable soups. Add chopped steamed veggies, and what do you think you have? Sure, vegetable chowder!!!!

The Amazing Cream of Potato Soup.

2 large russet potatoes, peeled and finely chopped
3 cups nonfat milk
1 cup vegetable broth
1 medium onion, finely chopped
$\frac{1}{2}$ tsp celery salt
1 tsp Nature's Seasonings
$\frac{1}{2}$ cup nonfat sour cream
2 tbsp chopped parsley
$\frac{1}{4}$ cup chopped green onion

In a pot, combine potatoes, milk, broth, onion, celery salt, and Nature's Seasonings. Bring to a boil. Lower heat and simmer until potatoes are tender. Remove from heat. Take half of the potatoes and broth and puree in a blender until smooth. Return to the pan and stir in sour cream. Serve sprinkled with parsley and green onions.

Nutritional:

Serving Size 9½ ounces
Servings per Recipe 6
Calories 125
Total Fat 0.544 gram
Saturated Fat 0.173 gram

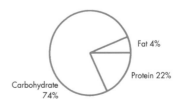

Fat 4%
Protein 22%
Carbohydrate 74%

Cream of Tomato Soup

The traditional when-you're-sick chicken soup has just been upstaged by this new and improved, perfect-when-you're-not-feeling-well-and-need-a-great-bowl-of-soothing-soup cream of tomato soup.

Made with fresh tomatoes, onions, carrots, potatoes, and light spices ... AAAHHH, just the thing to soothe and comfort you when you need it the most.

Let's rename it cream of comfort soup, your honor.

1 large onion, thinly sliced
5 cups vegetable bouillon
½ cup chopped carrots
½ cup peeled and chopped potatoes
8 large tomatoes, peeled, seeded, and cut into quarters
½ tsp sugar
¼ tsp white pepper
1 bay leaf
¾ tsp salt or Nature's Seasonings
½ tsp thyme
1 tsp parsley
2 cups nonfat sour cream

Sauté onion in a medium pot. Add broth, carrots, potatoes, tomatoes, and seasonings. Bring to a boil, lower the heat, and simmer 20–30 minutes, until carrots and potatoes are soft. Put soup in a blender and process until smooth. (You may have to do this in a few batches.) Stir in most of the sour cream. Serve with a dollop of sour cream on top.

Nutritional:

Serving Size 20 ounces
Servings per Recipe 6
Calories 141
Total Fat 1.72 grams
Saturated Fat 0.127 gram

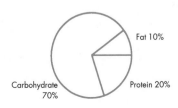

Fat 10%
Carbohydrate 70%
Protein 20%

Split Pea Soup

This is a sandwich soup—one of those great ham-hock-tasting soups that goes perfectly with a hoagie.

Of course, we took out the ham hock without taking out the ham hock flavor. (Do you think I've used the words "ham hock" enough in the last couple of sentences?) Anytime you feel like having soup is the best time for one of my favorites: The Ham-Hock-Tasting Without the Ham Hock Split Pea Soup!!!!!

2 cups dried split peas, green or yellow
2 quarts water or vegetable broth
1 cup finely chopped celery
1 medium onion, finely chopped
1 bay leaf
2 sprigs parsley
1 medium carrot, cut in quarters
4 slices uncooked turkey bacon

Place all ingredients in a pot. Bring to a boil, lower heat, and simmer for 1 hour, or until peas are tender. Remove turkey strips and discard. Put soup in a blender, reserving 1 cup of the peas. Blend until smooth. Add reserved peas and stir.

Garnish with a dollop of nonfat sour cream and croutons if desired.

Nutritional:

Serving Size 12 ounces
Servings per Recipe 8
Calories 202
Total Fat 1.63 grams
Saturated Fat 0.41 gram

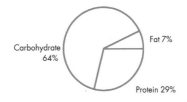

Carbohydrate 64%

Fat 7%

Protein 29%

Barley Soup

Our grain. Amber waves of barley (we need to add that) because we are second in the world in barley production (the former Soviet Union is first—we'll have to do something about that, but that's not a discussion for this book).

Barley Soup is great.

Serve it with hot Garlic Herb Bread (see page 212) sprinkled with Parmesan cheese and parsley.

Or with 2 cups of cooked sliced mushrooms or 1 cup of shredded zucchini—or both—thrown in to make this thicker and more nutritious.

Nothing like a bowl of great soup and this is one of them. Cook a bunch—this freezes well—and everyone loves it.

Warning on This One

This soup is best the day after you make it.

1 cup finely chopped onion
2 garlic cloves, chopped fine
½ cup dry whole barley
1 28-oz can chopped tomatoes
6 cups vegetable, chicken, or beef broth
1 cup finely chopped celery
1 cup carrots, cut into ¼-inch cubes
½ tsp celery salt
1 tsp Mrs. Dash
1 tsp Nature's Seasonings or Spike seasoning
1 Knorr bouillon cube
⅛ tsp white pepper
1 tsp dried thyme
2 tbsp chopped parsley

Sauté onion and garlic until limp. Add to other ingredients except parsley in a large stock pot. Bring to a boil, lower heat, and cook for 45 minutes to 1 hour. Sprinkle with parsley.

To make a beef barley soup, brown ½ pound lean sirloin, cut into 1-inch cubes. Remove beef from pan. Add onion and garlic to pan and follow recipe, adding beef with other ingredients.

Nutritional:

Serving Size 14 ounces
Servings per Recipe 7
Calories 126
Total Fat 1.97 grams
Saturated Fat 0.502 gram

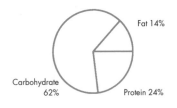

Fat 14%
Carbohydrate 62%
Protein 24%

Chicken Noodle Soup

Raise your American flag before you start cooking this because chicken noodle soup has earned its place right up there with baseball and apple pie.

What's the first thing you think of when you get sick? When you're tired, hungry, need some comfort? The first thing that comes to mind?

Visiting a friend who needs a big pot of . . . ?

Chicken noodle soup is everybody's favorite soup, and now you have the best, easiest chicken soup from scratch you could ever find.

 $\mathcal{F}$ab Ideas

Double or triple this one because the kids are going to devour it. Serve it anytime, anywhere, and with anything. . . . It's chicken noodle soup! What more needs to be said?

Oil for spray
6 pieces boneless, skinless chicken breast
1 medium onion, quartered
2 stalks celery, cut in half
2 carrots, quartered
1 tomato, left whole (for color and flavor)
1 clove garlic, minced
1 bay leaf
1/4 cup parsley
2 tsp Nature's Seasonings
3 14 1/2-oz cans defatted chicken broth
2 cups water
1 1/2 cups fine noodles broken into 2-inch pieces (angel hair pasta will do)

In a skillet sprayed with oil, brown chicken breasts well. Transfer to a soup pot and add onion, celery, carrots, tomato, garlic, bay leaf, parsley, and seasoning, and cover with the broth and water. Bring to a boil. Reduce heat and simmer, covered, for 1 hour. Remove vegetables and chicken. Cut up 5 chicken breast sections into bite-size pieces and return to pot (save the last piece for your favorite leftover chicken dish). Cut up the onions and carrots coarsely and return to pot. Throw away the garlic, tomato, celery, and parsley.

Add the noodles and simmer for 8–10 minutes or until the noodles are cooked.

Nutritional:

Serving Size 10 ounces
Servings per Recipe 10
Calories 160
Total Fat 2.05 grams
Saturated Fat 0.505 gram

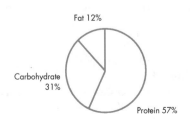

Fat 12%
Carbohydrate 31%
Protein 57%

Southwest Soup

Get out your best denim shirt,
Loads of silver,
Turquoise out the yin-yang,
And get ready to cook up some Southwest Soup.
With all the flavors of . . .

Chilies
Onions
Garlic

This is the one-dish-in-the-desert meal of all time 'cause there's so much you can do to it:

Throw in a can of black beans.
Have any kind of salad with it.

This turquoise-wearing gal likes a slice of Cornbread (see page 210)—add jalapeños, some fresh chopped cilantro, and a little nonfat cheddar cheese to the batter—with her Southwest Soup.

Kids

Soup Surprise.
Kids love this soup. No one woulda guessed it, but it's true.

Soup for Breakfast

Weird but true: Southwest Soup for breakfast. That's what our taste-testing women did and loved it!
Apparently it's Southwest Soup any time of the day or night.

2 cloves garlic, chopped
1 onion, chopped
1 lb boneless, skinless chicken breasts, cut into 1-inch pieces
1 28-oz can whole tomatoes

2 cans chicken broth
1 4-oz can whole chilies, chopped
½ cup mild taco sauce or salsa
1 tsp garlic powder
1 tsp onion powder
1 tsp Nature's Seasonings
1 tsp Mrs. Dash garlic and herb seasoning
½ cup white rice

Toppings
¼ cup chopped green onions
¼ cup chopped cilantro, if available
½ cup nonfat grated cheddar cheese
½ cup nonfat sour cream

Cook garlic and onion in nonstick pot for 3 minutes or until limp. Add remaining ingredients and cook for 15 minutes. Sprinkle soup with toppings and serve with tortilla chips (see recipe below).

Tortilla Chips

2 corn tortillas
Chili powder to taste
Salt and pepper to taste

Cut tortillas into 8 pieces each. Bake in 350-degree oven until brown, turn over, sprinkle with chili powder, salt, and pepper. Bake 5 minutes more. Serve with soup.

Nutritional:

Serving Size 8½ ounces
Servings per Recipe 8
Calories 212
Total Fat 5.3 grams
Saturated Fat 1.24 grams

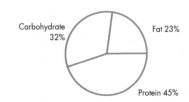

Carbohydrate 32%
Fat 23%
Protein 45%

Enough with the basic lettuce and tomato "that's all we can eat because I'm on a diet" salads of the past. FORGET ABOUT IT! Let's go wild. There isn't a salad in this book that could be listed as boring. If it didn't have some personality and great taste we didn't include it. Nothing ordinary for you, only things like:

> *Coconut Fruit Salad*
> *Confetti Coleslaw*
> *Wilted Cucumber Salad*
> *Twenty-four-hour Salad*
> *Oriental Cabbage Salad with Ramen*
> *Warm Chopped Summer Salad*
> *and on and on and on . . .*

So, TAKE THAT, lettuce, tomato, and lemon wedges of the past.

Salads and Dressings

Spinach Salad

The Past

Talk about a salad that up until now has needed a little PR. Take some spinach and bacon bits and tons of oil to make a high-fat spinach salad feast—but not anymore.

The Present

You can't get much better than fresh, loaded-with-vitamins spinach, egg whites, and crumbled turkey bacon topped off with Sweet-and-Sour Dressing (see page 74). Come on, this is the low-fat, all-American version of the old high-fat Italian (or wherever it originally came from), and it beats the heck out of any of those high-fat spinach salads of the past.

1 1/2 lb spinach, washed and stemmed
  4 hard-cooked egg whites, sliced
  4 slices turkey bacon, cooked and crumbled
    Sweet-and-Sour Dressing (see page 74) to taste

Combine all ingredients and serve immediately.

Nutritional:

Serving Size 4 1/2 ounces
Servings per Recipe 8
Calories 63
Total Fat 1.30 grams
Saturated Fat 0.381 gram

Carbohydrate 34%
Fat 17%
Alcohol (dressing) 7%
Protein 42%

Wilted Cucumber Salad

Wilted used to mean

limp
sad
saggy
sacky (sacky being a new word?)

Now wilted means a fabulous-tasting cucumber salad that's as refreshing as a cool breeze, light and tasty as . . . a wilted cucumber salad, and the perfect quick-and-easy salad to chow down on when you're dying for something . . . I don't know, something . . .
WILTED
That's it.
Something wilted.

3 medium cucumbers
1 small red onion, cut in half and thinly sliced
3/4 cup rice vinegar
1/8 tsp white pepper
1 tbsp sugar
   Salt and pepper to taste

Peel and slice cucumbers very thin. Layer cucumbers with salt in a covered container for 1 hour. Pour off accumulated liquid, rinse cucumbers, and drain well.

Combine vinegar and remaining ingredients. Pour over cucumbers and onions.

Serve with sour cream, dill, or parsley sprinkled on top.

Nutritional:

Serving Size 6
Servings per Recipe 6 ounces
Calories 30
Total Fat 0.197 gram
Saturated Fat 0.065 gram

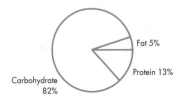

Fat 5%

Protein 13%

Carbohydrate
82%

Warm Chopped Summer Salad

Ahhhhh . . . a refreshing salad with wonderful flavor. Serve it with toasted Garlic Herb Bread (see page 212), and it is good enough to call a meal.

Or it goes just as well alongside any dish for which you need a salad to dress up. There's nothing like this chopped summer number when you're hankering for a salad.

1 tsp olive oil
2 cloves garlic, chopped
1 red bell pepper, seeded and diced
1/2 lb mushrooms, sliced
1 stalk broccoli (about 1/4 lb), stem peeled and sliced, head broken into small florets
1/2 cauliflower (about 1/2 lb), broken into small florets
1/4 cup vegetable broth
2 medium zucchini, coarsely shredded
1 yellow squash, coarsely shredded
3 ripe tomatoes, chopped
1/2 cup frozen petite corn
2 green onions, chopped
2 tbsp Italian parsley
1 tbsp fresh basil
2 tsp Nature's Seasonings
1 tsp Mrs. Dash garlic herb mix
2 tbsp lemon juice

In a large pan place olive oil, garlic, red bell pepper, mushrooms, broccoli, and cauliflower. Cook over medium to high heat for 3–5 minutes or until vegetables are just tender. Add vegetable broth. Cook 3 minutes more. Add remaining ingredients and simmer on medium low for 3 minutes more.

Nutritional:

Serving Size 8 ounces
Servings per Recipe 6
Calories 77
Total Fat 1.43 grams
Saturated Fat 0.197 gram

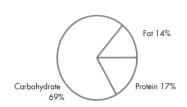

Fat 14%
Protein 17%
Carbohydrate 69%

Confetti Coleslaw

As American as baseball, but it has never gotten the credit. Do you see a catcher's mitt in every deli across the country? I don't think so.

If this wasn't so low in fat, the color alone in this purple-and-corn salad would be enough to win a prize (and the corn is the very thing, I might add, that ambushes the cabbage enough to get the kids to eat it).

Swear.

Consider this artwork.

Think creative. Think color.

Take this to the next wedding you go to and throw it at the bride. She'll thank you for it after she has a couple of kids and is looking around for a great low-fat coleslaw recipe.

*P*ssssst . . .

Present it as an addition to any sandwich under the sun.

A side dish to every dish I can think of . . . It's Barbecue Helper at its best.

Everything and coleslaw, that's what I think of when I think of slaw.

3 cups thinly shredded Chinese (Napa) cabbage
1 cup thinly shredded purple cabbage
1 red bell pepper, with seeds removed and thinly sliced
1½ cups corn (frozen is okay)
½ tsp dry mustard
½ tsp white pepper
½ tsp celery salt
1 tbsp sugar
½ cup seasoned rice vinegar
½ cup nonfat mayonnaise

Combine ingredients, chill, and serve.

Nutritional:

Serving Size 4 ounces
Servings per Recipe 6
Calories 60
Total Fat 0.315 gram
Saturated Fat 0.037 gram

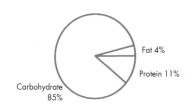

Fat 4%

Protein 11%

Carbohydrate
85%

Oriental Cabbage Salad with Ramen

I'm going to take a stand on this Ramen issue. (You didn't even know there was a Ramen issue going on in our country, did you?) We invented those little Ramen packages that you see in every supermarket in the country, and we invented the supermarkets. So there: Ramen noodles are American.

If you've been within a ten-mile radius of a school function in the last five years, you've seen this dish. It's the one in the huge bowl that always runs out first because everyone loves it. I've bagged the almonds and sesame seeds—otherwise known as the fat. They're OUTTA HERE, and I've added fresh flavors and other healthy stuff.

Think:

> Summertime
> Cold
> Refreshing
> Barbecue
> Romantic picnic (yeah, when's the last time you went on one of those?)
> Kid's party
> A great big bowl of it in the fridge for you to snack on anytime.
> And think American whenever you think Ramen Noodles.

1 package oriental-flavor ramen noodle soup (low-fat)
¹/₂ medium cabbage, shredded
4 scallions, cut into small circles

Dressing
¹/₄ cup apple juice
1 tbsp soy sauce
2 tbsp sugar
1 tsp minced ginger
1¹/₂ tbsp rice vinegar
¹/₂ tsp salt
¹/₄ tsp pepper

2 tbsp grated carrot for garnish

Prepare ramen noodles according to package directions, then let cool.

Combine cabbage and scallions. Add dressing and toss to mix.

Add cooled noodle mixture and toss again.

Garnish with grated carrots.

Nutritional:

Serving Size 3¹/₂ ounces
Servings per Recipe 6
Calories 70
Total Fat 0.49 gram
Saturated Fat 0.046 gram

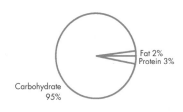

Fat 2%
Protein 3%

Carbohydrate
95%

Red Potato Salad

Potato salad and

Fourth of July
Fried chicken
Corn on the cob
Late-night snacking

Potato salad and anything!
Plain or . . .
Add some crumbled turkey bacon = German Potato Salad
A little curry = Indian Potato Salad

Not much is better than good old American potato salad!

3 lb small red potatoes, cut in half
2 stalks celery, thinly sliced
¼ cup thinly sliced red onion
¼ cup seasoned rice vinegar
¼ cup low-fat mayonnaise
½ cup nonfat sour cream
¼ cup chopped parsley
½ tsp celery salt
½ tsp white pepper

Place potatoes in a large pot, cover with water, and bring to a boil. Cook until tender, 15–20 minutes (depending on size of potatoes). Drain and run cold water over them to cool. Add remaining ingredients, chill, and serve.

Nutritional:

Serving Size 10 ounces
Servings per Recipe 6
Calories 195
Total Fat 2.37 grams
Saturated Fat 0.434 gram

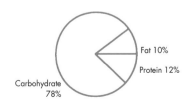

Fat 10%

Protein 12%

Carbohydrate 78%

Three Bean Salad

Throw this together and put it in the fridge. You can eat it all week—this salad lasts forever.

It's cool.

It's refreshing.

It's a great hot summer salad or a good cold-night-by-the-fire-with-someone-you-love salad. Beans and someone you *really* love and someone who *really* loves you.

It's a picnic classic . . .

A deli manager's dream . . .

And an all-around great salad!

1 lb French-cut frozen green beans, thawed
1 15-oz can garbanzo beans, drained and rinsed
1 15-oz can red kidney beans, drained and rinsed
1/2 cup minced red onion
1/3 cup chopped parsley
2 cloves garlic, minced
1 tsp Nature's Seasonings or salt
1 tsp dried basil
3/4 cup rice vinegar

Drain green beans. Combine with remaining ingredients in a container with a lid. Refrigerate, turning over occasionally. This will keep in the refrigerator for a week.

Nutritional:

Serving Size 9 ounces
Servings per Recipe 6
Calories 177
Total Fat 1.22 grams
Saturated Fat 0.151 gram

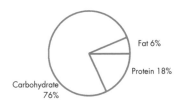

Fat 6%

Protein 18%

Carbohydrate 76%

Tomato and Green Bean Salad

It's your choice on this one. You can stay with this basic, great-tasting tomato and green bean salad that works perfectly as a summer veggie dish or a perfect salad to accompany rice or a baked potato . . .

Or you can . . .

Drain a can of tuna, chop up some cooked egg whites, grab your beret, open up a loaf of French bread, and go to town with the dressed-up version of this salad.

Either way, you're gonna love it.

1 lb fresh green beans, with tips removed
2 large ripe tomatoes, thinly sliced
2 garlic cloves, crushed
2 green onions, finely chopped
1/4 cup seasoned rice vinegar
1/2 tsp fresh ground pepper
1/2 tsp salt
1 tsp fresh marjoram

Put beans in a pot in 1 inch of boiling water. Cover and steam for 5 minutes, or until crisp and tender. Drain and rinse with cold water until no longer hot. Place in a salad bowl with tomatoes, garlic, and onions. Pour on rice vinegar, sprinkle spices over, and toss. Chill and serve.

For Salade Niçoise, add:

1 6-oz can water-packed albacore tuna
2 hard-cooked egg whites, chopped
1 small jar water-packed artichoke hearts

Nutritional:

Serving Size 5 ounces
Servings per Recipe 6
Calories 45
Total Fat 0.316 gram
Saturated Fat 0.051 gram

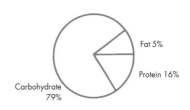

Fat 5%

Protein 16%

Carbohydrate 79%

Cobb Salad

This is the kind of salad you grab from the fridge, put in your lap, and sit with the whole bowl in front of you while you watch a great tearjerker movie on TV.

A bed of lettuce, mounds of chopped egg white, tomatoes, green onions, avocado (just a touch), low-fat cheese, turkey, turkey bacon, topped with a garlic vinaigrette (or any other dressing in this mix-and-match kind of cookbook) . . . could anything be better than that for dinner in front of a movie???

8 cups torn lettuce greens (a mix of red leaf, romaine, and
 iceberg is nice)
1½ cups smoked or oven-roasted nonfat turkey, cut into thin
 strips
2 cups coarsely chopped tomatoes
1½ cups sliced hard-cooked egg whites
2 tbsp crumbled blue cheese
1½ cups finely chopped nonfat Monterey Jack cheese
½ cup finely chopped green onions
2 tbsp diced avocado
6 slices turkey bacon, cooked and crumbled

Place a bed of torn lettuce on a large serving platter. Place
turkey on top of the greens. Mound the tomatoes at one end
and the egg whites at the other. Combine the blue cheese
with the Monterey Jack cheese and mound next to the tomatoes. Mound the green onions next to the egg whites. Scatter
the avocado and crumbled bacon over the turkey.

Another way to serve is to mound the turkey in the middle
of the greens and scatter the avocado and bacon over the
turkey. Place the tomatoes, cheeses, onions, and egg whites
in concentric circles around the turkey.

Serve Creamy Herb Vinaigrette (see page 70) on the side.

Nutritional:

Serving Size 5½ ounces
Servings per Recipe 8
Calories 111
Total Fat 2.83 grams
Saturated Fat 0.984 gram

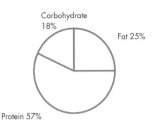

Carbohydrate 18%
Fat 25%
Protein 57%

Waldorf Salad

Time for a field trip to New York to stand in front of The Waldorf-Astoria hotel on Park Avenue and give a salute, and THANK YOU BUT NO THANK YOU for your old high-fat version of this little salad.

We've taken this creamy, sweet, crunchy fresh fruit salad (minus the nuts and high-fat mayo) and made it perfect for all holiday meals or as a plain old great afternoon snack for the kids.

 ssssst . . .

 Waldorf secret: Stick this in front of anyone with a couple of Oatmeal Raisin Cookies (see page 298) and call it dessert. See if you get any protests . . .

2 tsp rice vinegar
$\frac{1}{4}$ cup nonfat sour cream
$\frac{1}{4}$ cup nonfat mayonnaise
1 tsp honey
3 cups cored and chopped apples
1 cup halved seedless grapes
2 cups mini marshmallows
1 cup chopped celery
$\frac{1}{2}$ cup raisins

Combine vinegar, sour cream, mayonnaise, and honey. Toss with other ingredients and serve on shredded lettuce.

Nutritional:

Serving Size 5 ounces
Servings per Recipe 6
Calories 157
Total Fat 0.467 gram
Saturated Fat 0.109 gram

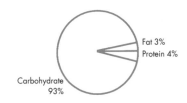

Fat 3%
Protein 4%
Carbohydrate 93%

Coconut Fruit Salad

If you're hankering for something light, creamy, and sweet, desserty or side dishy, something that works as well as a side dish for grilled fish as it does for your late-night snack food, a breakfast food, or an eat-it-in-the-car food . . . then you're in luck. Not only is Coconut Fruit Salad perfect for all of the above, it will also be a winner in the battle of the non-fruit-eating kid.

This is also the dish that will win at any potluck school event.

You know good and well that you always run into the deli department of your local grocery store minutes before you're supposed to be at one of those potluck things and pick up some kind of deli tray, feeling as guilty as sin because you just can't seem to get it together to make your own.

Well, I've got the answer for you. Something easy, easy, easy that you can make, and THIS IS A WINNER.

Crafty Suggestions from Me:

Decorate the sides of the dish with a replica of the school building!

Stick small American flags in your winner potluck dish. That'll get 'em every time!

You wanna upstage everybody there? Grab yourself a watermelon. Scoop it out and plunk your fruit salad in nature's bowl, if you know what I mean. Take that to the potluck dinner, knowing good and well that you've won before you even walk through the door.

1 20-oz can (2½ cups) pineapple chunks in natural juice,
   drained
1 11-oz can mandarin oranges, drained
½ cup halved red seedless grapes
½ cup halved green seedless grapes
1 Granny Smith apple, peeled and diced
1 cup miniature marshmallows
1 tsp coconut extract or flavoring
1½ cups nonfat sour cream
1 tbsp flaked coconut

Mix together all ingredients except flaked coconut. Sprinkle
the flaked coconut over the top of the salad and enjoy.

Nutritional:

Serving Size 7 ounces
Servings per Recipe 8
Calories 134
Total Fat 0.46 gram
Saturated Fat 0.238 gram

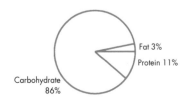

Fat 3%
Protein 11%
Carbohydrate 86%

Twenty-four-hour Salad

No need to thank me. We've taken this fabulous traditional loaded-with-fat, creamy fruit salad and defatted the hell out of it.

Make this baby the night before (notice the twenty-four-hour reference in the title) and chill until the next day. You'll see how good the grapes, pineapple, oranges, cantaloupe, honeydew melon, cherries, blueberries, bananas, and nectarines taste mixed together and chilled.

Everyone loves this dish. There shouldn't be a picnic or potluck without it.

Kids

All you gotta do to get the kids asking for more is throw in a few (only a few) marshmallows and call it dessert.

1 egg, beaten
2 egg whites, beaten
2 tbsp sugar
4 tbsp orange juice
2 tbsp rice vinegar
1 tbsp reduced-fat margarine
   Pinch of salt
16 oz nonfat sour cream
1 cup red and green seedless grapes
1½ cups chopped pineapple or 1 15-oz can pineapple chunks
1 cup chopped orange (1 small orange)
1 cup cantaloupe or honeydew melon chunks (½ melon)
1 cup pitted cherries
½ cup blueberries
1 cup sliced banana or ½ cup dried bananas (1 large banana)
1 cup sliced nectarines
1 cup mini marshmallows

In a small saucepan, stir the egg and egg whites, sugar, orange juice, and vinegar over medium-low heat until just thickened. Remove from heat and stir in margarine and salt. Let cool.

Fold the cooled mixture into the sour cream.

Combine fruit and marshmallows in a large bowl. Pour mixture over fruit and stir until the fruit is coated with the dressing. Chill, covered, overnight.

Nutritional:

Serving Size 4 ounces
Servings per Recipe 16
Calories 90
Total Fat 1.02 grams
Saturated Fat 0.229 gram

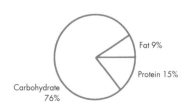

Fat 9%

Protein 15%

Carbohydrate 76%

Herb Croutons

A crouton shouldn't be fattening.
A crouton should be low-fat and ready . . .

. . . anytime you want to throw something on top of a salad.

. . . the minute you're in the mood to splash spicy and crunchy all over your cream of tomato soup.

. . . on hand to eat while you're driving all over town.

. . . as a handy snack until you can make it to lunch or dinner.

. . . whenever you need a dressing for your best casserole.

It's time we got the fat out and the crouton back in—into everything!!!

1 small loaf French or sourdough bread, with crust removed
and cut into 1-inch squares
1 tsp *each* dried parsley, oregano, basil, garlic powder, onion
powder
½ tsp celery salt
1 tsp Mrs. Dash
Olive oil spray

Preheat oven to 375 degrees.

Combine dry spices in a plastic bag large enough to hold the croutons. Spray croutons very lightly with olive oil spray and toss in spice mixture. Place on cookie sheet and bake until chewy crisp, about 30 minutes. Store in a plastic bag in freezer or refrigerator.

Nutritional:

Serving Size 1 ounce
Servings per Recipe 9
Calories 73
Total Fat 0.823 gram
Saturated Fat 0.172 gram

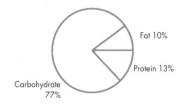

Fat 10%

Protein 13%

Carbohydrate
77%

Creamy Herb Vinaigrette

Couldn't do a cookbook without this recipe because who can have salads in their lives without a good Herb Vinaigrette? This one has it all, except the fat.

There are very few low-fat herb vinaigrette dressings out there that don't taste gross but with this you can get the taste without the usual ½ cup of oil/fat.

A dressing that'll make you proud—and leaner.

This is really good, with just a touch of olive oil and lots of fresh basil, vinegar, garlic, and spices. You can pour it over your favorite salad or use it as a dip for fresh cucumbers and bell peppers. Expect a zingy, strong herb vinaigrette flavor without all the fat.

$^1/_3$ cup rice vinegar
$^1/_2$ tsp olive oil
2 tbsp nonfat sour cream
1 clove garlic
$^1/_2$ tsp Nature's Seasonings
$^1/_2$ tsp Mrs. Dash onion and herb mix
$1^1/_2$ tsp dried basil or 6 fresh basil leaves
2 tbsp Italian parsley

Combine all ingredients in blender.

Nutritional:

Serving Size 2 ounces/$^1/_4$ cup
Servings per Recipe 2
Calories 28.9
Total Fat 1.17 grams
Saturated Fat 0.16 gram

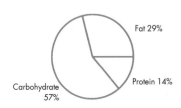

Fat 29%

Protein 14%

Carbohydrate 57%

Caesar Dressing

I'm stumped by this one. Everywhere I go people are ordering Caesar salad, and what is it? Romaine lettuce with dressing. Why do millions of people in every coffee shop and restaurant in the country order this amazingly high-fat salad?

Check it out. Caesar dressing is loaded—90% fat!

If you're getting all that fat for a little Romaine lettuce, why not defat it and improve the taste a bit?

So I did. HA, HA.

Taste test this one with your friends. Give them the Caesar test. Drop a hint at your local Frenchy, Caesar-salad-serving restaurant.

You'll be a hometown hero (suggest a parade; ticker tape is good). Grand prizes for you and your friends, and a reign of at least a year to all the people who are saving 7 grams of fat every time they eat this salad.

4 tbsp lemon juice
2 cloves garlic
1 tsp olive oil
4 anchovy fillets, rinsed
2 tbsp nonfat Parmesan cheese
2 tbsp nonfat sour cream
1 tsp Nature's Seasonings
1 tsp Mrs. Dash garlic and herb mix

Combine all ingredients in a blender.

Serve over fresh torn romaine lettuce with Herb Croutons (see page 68).

Nutritional:

Serving Size 1 ounce/2 tbsp
Servings per Recipe 5
Calories 34
Total Fat 1.26 grams
Saturated Fat 0.201 gram

Fat 30%

Carbohydrate 39%

Protein 31%

Sweet-and-Sour Dressing

Now, excuse me. Put six things in a blender and come up with something that tastes this good?

Easy? Did I promise you easy?

Garlic, honey, rice vinegar, and spices: YUUUMMM.

You'll never not have anything on hand to dress your salads (or anything else) again.

2 cloves garlic, minced
1 tbsp honey
½ cup seasoned rice vinegar
½ cup rice wine (mirin)
1 tsp Dijon mustard
1 tsp Spike seasoning

Combine all ingredients in a blender. Use on Spinach Salad
(see page 44) or as a topping for steamed veggies.

Nutritional:

Serving Size 2½ ounces/¼ cup
Servings per Recipe 4
Calories 56.8
Total Fat 0.025 gram
Saturated Fat 0.007 gram

Carbohydrate 65%

Fat less than 1%
Protein 3%

Alcohol 31%

Green Goddess Dressing

If you love to dip—and I do—then dip into this.

Fresh garlic, anchovy, chives, lemon, parsley, mayo, and sour cream, with just the right spices.

The Green Goddess doesn't just serve up well as your basic dip, it solves the age-old question: What do I put on my baked potato? (Did you know that was an age-old question?)

Add the goddess to anything that needs dipping or topping with something tasty, or to any salad that has to have something creamy on top!

1 clove garlic, minced
1 tbsp anchovy paste, or 2 anchovy fillets, rinsed and chopped
4 tbsp chopped chives or green onion
2 tbsp lemon juice
2 tbsp white wine vinegar
1 cup nonfat mayonnaise
1/2 cup nonfat sour cream
1/3 cup chopped parsley
3 tbsp nonfat milk
1/4 tsp pepper, preferably freshly ground

Blend all ingredients. Refrigerate.

Nutritional:

Serving Size 2 ounces/1/4 cup
Servings per Recipe 8
Calories 31
Total Fat 0.14 gram
Saturated Fat 0.03 gram

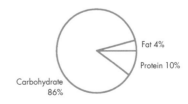

Fat 4%

Protein 10%

Carbohydrate 86%

Ginger Garlic Soy Lime Dressing

The longest named dressing in the country and it isn't meant for weenies. You gotta love robust, strong flavors to love this, and I do.

*I*deas from the Chef

Make up a batch and serve it over any grilled fish, chicken, steamed veggies, or rice and you'll see what I mean.

If you're a weenie but want to test the waters, dilute it with a little rice vinegar or water and serve over a romaine or spinach salad. . . .

Exotic weenie? Same thing, only add some mandarin oranges.

1 cup tamari or light soy sauce
4 tbsp rice vinegar
¼ cup lime juice
8 small to medium garlic cloves
2 tbsp fresh grated ginger or 1 tsp dried ginger
1½ tbsp Spike seasoning
1½ tsp dark sesame oil
¼ tsp chili oil

Combine all ingredients in a blender. Pulse until garlic is chopped fine.

Nutritional:

Serving Size 1 ounce/2 tbsp
Servings per Recipe 4½
Calories 16
Total Fat 0.255 gram
Saturated Fat 0.034 gram

Fat 12%

Carbohydrate 55%

Protein 33%

French Dressing

Ha! French, my butt. Why'd they get the credit for one of America's favorites? I say we reclaim it, and what better way to take it back than make it better than it ever was?

Now you've got it. Fat-free, delicious, OURS. Dippable and pourable on everything.

¼ cup rice vinegar
¼ cup V-8 juice
2 tbsp lemon juice
¾ tsp dry mustard
½ tsp salt
¼ tsp paprika
4 tbsp nonfat mayonnaise
1 tsp sugar
Pinch of cayenne

Mix all ingredients together and chill.

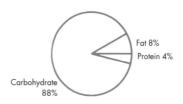

Nutritional:

Serving Size 1 ounce/2 tbsp
Servings per Recipe 4
Calories 25
Total Fat 0.25 gram
Saturated Fat 0.028 gram

Fat 8%
Protein 4%
Carbohydrate 88%

Thousand Island Dressing

The famous, the worldly, the highest fat in the land is no more. If this doesn't taste like your favorite high-fat-of-the-past Thousand Island Dressing at 6 grams of fat per TABLE-SPOON, then I'll get the hell out of the cookbook-writing business because I'd stake my reputation (just like the cowboys of the old West) that you can smear this all over your burger, dip your fries into it, and pour it all over your favorite salad and never, ever miss all the fat that you used to get just doing some dressing.

1 cup nonfat mayonnaise
¼ cup chili sauce
3 hard-cooked egg whites, chopped
2 tbsp finely chopped celery
2 tbsp finely chopped onion
1 tbsp sweet relish
½ tsp salt
½ tsp paprika

Mix all ingredients well and refrigerate.

Nutritional:

Serving Size 1 ounce/2 tbsp
Servings per Recipe 10
Calories 32.6
Total Fat 0.05 gram
Saturated Fat 0.009 gram

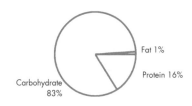

Fat 1%

Protein 16%

Carbohydrate
83%

ENTREE means come on in.
C'mon America, Let's Eat: *see the connection?*

*Come on in and eat with us. It's a new day.
I'm not talking sunup to sunset, I'm talking
about the millions of women all over the greatest
country in the world who are never gonna diet
again. You know it doesn't work because it
didn't. You, me, and millions of our friends
gained the weight back every time we lost it, and
since we ain't gonna diet again, then we've got
to eat.*

*Eat to fuel our bodies.
Eat to have the energy and strength to live
our lives.
Eat to live.*

But eat what?
I've got the answer . . . EAT THIS.

*Meatloaf
Chili Cornbread Pie
Chicken with Garlic Sauce
Zucchini Cheese Pie
Etc.*

*Eat your favorite foods. Enjoy the tastes you love
most. Make it easy: convenient for your busy
schedule but without the fat. Who needs it? And,
finally, YOU CAN LIVE WITHOUT IT. C'mon
America, Let's Eat!*

Entrees

Chicken with Mushrooms and Pasta

Your new Chicken with Mushrooms and Pasta dish restores the good name of every heavy cream sauce or Alfredo-y chicken dish of the past. This is a better version of the old Italian chicken dishes. (I'm sure to end up at the bottom of a river for even suggesting that, but sorry, Don—and I'm not talking Don Smith here, I'm talking THE DON, as in the head of a Family kind of Don.)

This dish was born to impress—the boss, the almost in-laws, the new flame, the Perfect Moms Club. You see, it's so easy and fools them into believing every time that you've been cooking all day.

Take full credit. Say that by the time you marinated it in wine, found just the right mush-rooms, and added the herbs, you had very little time left but man-aged to finish embroidering the border of the tablecloth they're eating on anyway.

What the hell, go for it. They'll be too busy loving their Chicken with Mushrooms and Pasta to question.

Marinade
- ⅓ **cup white wine**
- 1 **tsp lemon juice**
- 1 **tsp basil**
- ½ **tsp oregano**
- ½ **tsp garlic powder**
- ¼ **tsp salt**
  pinch of pepper

3–4 **oz boneless, skinless chicken breasts**
1 **tbsp olive oil**

½ cup chopped onion
5 garlic cloves, minced
2 medium portobello mushrooms, cut into thin strips
½ tsp thyme
1 tbsp flour
¼ tsp nutmeg
1 tsp salt
¼ tsp pepper
1 12-oz can evaporated skim milk
½ cup chicken broth
12 oz penne, cooked according to package directions
2 tbsp chopped parsley

Combine marinade ingredients and marinate chicken for 1–2 hours. Heat oven to 350 degrees.

Bake chicken in marinade for 15–20 minutes, until juices run clear. Remove chicken, cool, and cut into strips. Reserve cooking juices.

Heat oil in a nonstick skillet. Sauté onion and garlic until soft. Add mushrooms and continue cooking for 3–4 minutes, until released juices have been reabsorbed.

Add flour and cook for a few seconds. Add chicken drippings, thyme, nutmeg, salt, pepper, and milk. Cook until everything is heated through. Add chicken broth and adjust seasoning. Add chicken strips and heat through.

Serve over cooked penne and decorate with chopped parsley.

Nutritional:

Serving Size 16 ounces
Servings per Recipe 4
Calories 480
Total Fat 6.06 grams
Saturated Fat 1.09 grams

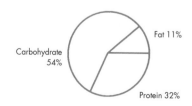

Fat 11%
Carbohydrate 54%
Protein 32%

Chicken with Dijon and Apricot Sauce

You're wondering if I've gone mad, aren't you?

An all-American cookbook with a Chicken with Dijon and Apricot Sauce recipe in it?

Well, let me tell ya, I'm scanning the all-American best: Betty's, the best of *Houses and Porches*, and the greatest *Housekeeping*s. Everywhere I look I see some kind of curry dish. I think: Curry from India? No connection at all with the spacious skies, amber waves of grain, purple mountain majesties, or fruited plains. But apparently Americans like curry, although I've never met an American who invited me over for some. Now, mustard I understand. Think hot dog, think ballpark. I get that. I one-upped them all with our nineties version of a Dijon dish, with a splash of curry.

Other than my upstaging Betty, this dish had all the components to make it into this book: a potluck kind of dish, great tasting, easy, impressive, something you can serve over anything.

Keep it simple: over rice, pasta, a baked potato.

Romance

Hey, you and the lover on India night? Why not work it into the bedroom, if you know what I mean . . .

Come on, ladies, grab your sarongs and dance into that bedroom with a little Dijon dish: spice it up!!!!

1 tbsp vegetable oil
4 4-oz boneless, skinless chicken breasts
1 cup chopped onion
2 cloves garlic, minced
½ cup chicken broth
1 tsp curry powder
2 tbsp Dijon-style mustard
½ cup apricot preserves
½ cup nonfat plain yogurt
  Salt and pepper to taste

Heat oil over medium-high heat in a nonstick skillet. Sauté chicken until browned, about 3–5 minutes per side. Remove from pan and set aside.

Lower heat and in the same skillet sauté onion and garlic until soft. Add 1–2 tablespoons chicken broth if necessary to keep it moist.

Add curry powder, mustard, apricot preserves, and remaining broth. Cook for 10 minutes. Return chicken with juices to pan and continue cooking 8–10 minutes, until juices run clear.

Add yogurt (at room temperature), salt, and pepper. Heat through and serve over rice.

Nutritional:

Serving Size 10 ounces
Servings per Recipe 4
Calories 305
Total Fat 5.17 grams
Saturated Fat 0.688 gram

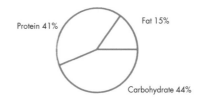

Protein 41%   Fat 15%   Carbohydrate 44%

Oven Barbecued Chicken

Think tasty, just off the grill, very quick and easy. Don't think crispy, don't think fried, because it's not fried, because it's not fried chicken (got that for you on page 92). This is oven barbecued. Definitely think *double* because it's one of the best leftovers dishes you've ever tasted.

Sauce

- 1 cup tomato juice
- 1/3 cup cider vinegar
- 1 1/2 tsp salt
- 1/2 tsp red pepper flakes or Tabasco
- 1 tbsp Dijon mustard
- 2 tbsp lemon juice
- 2 tbsp brown sugar
- 2 tbsp Worcestershire sauce
- 1/2 cup ketchup

- 1 large onion, sliced (about 2 cups)
- 6 large garlic cloves, minced
- 2 large bay leaves
- 8 8-oz skinless chicken breasts (bone in)

Preheat oven to 300 degrees.

In a bowl, combine all sauce ingredients.

In a baking pan large enough to accommodate the chicken in one layer, spread out onion, garlic, and bay leaves.

Lay chicken on top and ladle sauce on generously.

Bake in a 300-degree oven for 45 minutes to 1 hour, or until juices run clear.

If you would like the sauce to be thicker, remove the chicken to a platter to keep warm and place sauce under broiler until it bubbles and onions turn golden brown.

Pour sauce over chicken and enjoy!

Nutritional:

Serving Size 7 ounces
Servings per Recipe 8
Calories 177
Total Fat 1.6 grams
Saturated Fat 0.408 gram

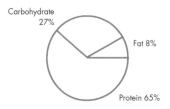

Carbohydrate 27%
Fat 8%
Protein 65%

Oven-fried Chicken

It's time to cuss out the Colonel.

Sorry, but the minute you taste this oven-fried chicken, you'll march right down to the Colonel's headquarters and cuss him up, down, and sideways. All these years you've been chowing down on 52% fat in one measly drumstick!

$\mathcal{T}$hings to Do with a Drumstick:

Stumble to the fridge, pull out a leg, and chow down.
Dump some salsa on cold chicken and chow down.
Rip it off the bone, throw it between two slices of bread with some ketchup, and chow down.

Once you wake up and feel a tad more civilized:

Cut it up and make a chicken salad, low-fat everything else.
Burritos? Of course.
Anything that has to do with a picnic, you're in.
Fry it up, nonstick pan, and you've got an omelet stuffing.
Unfry wings and open a bar.
Unfry a drumstick and join a band.
Unfry the gizzards and pick up a banjo.

2 cups bread crumbs
1 tsp Nature's Seasonings or Spike seasoning
1 tsp onion herb mixture
1 tsp garlic powder
$^1/_4$ tsp white pepper
$^1/_2$ tsp celery salt
2 egg whites, lightly beaten
1 cup nonfat yogurt
3 lb skinless defatted chicken pieces (thighs, legs, and breasts)
1 cup flour
  Nonfat margarine spray

Preheat oven to 425 degrees.

Combine bread crumbs with spices. Combine egg whites with yogurt.

Roll chicken pieces in flour, then in yogurt, then in bread crumbs, coating thoroughly.

Put chicken in a shallow baking dish. Spray chicken very lightly with margarine and bake for 35–40 minutes, or until crisp.

Nutritional:

Serving Size 6$^1/_2$ ounces
Servings per Recipe 8
Calories 364
Total Fat 8.59 grams
Saturated Fat 2.3 grams

Carbohydrate 38%

Fat 22%

Protein 40%

Chicken Paprika

I know, I know. You're thinking: Paprika—gross.

Who even knows what to do with this spice? You hear about it, but have you ever really used it? Maybe once a year you put some paprika in soup.

Before this cookbook came out, this dish had a Hungarian history to it. But forget that. Our only reference is to hungry, and that is how you should feel before you eat this dish because it's good and satisfying and red, white, and blue through and through.

Food for Thought

This is a "throw over" dish. That is, throw it over . . .

Noodles
Rice
Steamed fresh veggies

Like a good American quilt, throw it over anything and enjoy.

Or try a cold chicken sandwich with sliced red peppers, lettuce and cucumber, and nonfat mayo.

6 large boneless, skinless chicken breasts
1 tbsp Hungarian paprika
$^1/_2$ tsp salt
$^1/_4$ tsp white pepper
$^1/_2$ tsp garlic powder
1 $^1/_2$ cups defatted chicken broth
$^3/_4$ cup nonfat sour cream
   Bowtie noodles
$^1/_4$ cup chopped parsley

In a nonstick skillet over high heat, brown chicken breasts about 2 minutes on each side, then remove from pan.

Add spices to pan and stir 1 minute. Add chicken broth and cook for 5 minutes, reducing liquid slightly.

Turn heat to low and add sour cream. Return chicken to pan and simmer for 3 minutes, covered, or until chicken is cooked through.

Serve over bowtie noodles and sprinkle with parsley.

Nutritional:

Serving Size 6 ounces
Servings per Recipe 6
Calories 172
Total Fat 3.11 grams
Saturated Fat 0.845 gram

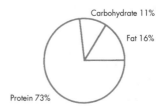

Carbohydrate 11%

Fat 16%

Protein 73%

Chicken Fricassee

I've stolen this from the French and given it American citizenship because there is a life-and-death situation going on here, and we've saved the day.

It's a Purple Heart,

Medal of Honor,

Silver Star kind of thing because . . .

This traditional French dish used to be loaded with fat, and we here at the Susan Powter Let's Eat America Kitchen have defatted the hell out of it, therefore saving lives.

What do you think? Doesn't saving millions of lives constitute a reason for this dish becoming American? Please check with any veteran on this one.

This is the big supper kind of meal.

Sunday best.

Served over noodles or dumplings.

Fancy Schmancy

Serve it over wild rice—still simple but with a touch of class.

If you're looking for sheer elegance, listen to this: Chicken Fricassee served over wild rice with steamed fresh asparagus, then Chocolate Orange Cake (see page 320) and Black Chocolate Sauce (see page 346).

Get out the ball gown before you serve that one.

Either way, this is a lifesaving good looker of a dish.

    Nonstick spray
12 skinless chicken pieces
 1 lb mushrooms, sliced
 1 medium onion, sliced
 1 tbsp minced garlic

½ cup white wine (optional)
4 cups chicken broth
4 tbsp cornstarch
½ tsp celery salt
¼ tsp white pepper
½ tsp marjoram
½ tsp thyme
1¼ cups nonfat sour cream
3 tbsp fresh chopped parsley

Brown chicken over high heat in deep sauté pan or dutch oven coated with nonstick spray. Remove chicken to a platter.

Add onion, mushrooms, and garlic to same pan and cook for at least 3 minutes, or until vegetables are soft.

If you are using wine, add it now and cook over high heat 1 minute.

Add 3 cups of broth, and bring to a boil. Reduce the heat to a simmer.

Combine the cornstarch* with the remaining cup of broth, mixing thoroughly. Add to pan and stir until broth thickens slightly.

Return chicken to pan and cook until chicken is cooked through, about 15 minutes.

Remove from heat and add the spices and sour cream.

Serve with Green Onion Dumplings (see recipe on page 170) and sprinkle with parsley.

Nutritional:

Serving Size 11 ounces
Servings per Recipe 8
Calories 214
Total Fat 5.06 grams
Saturated Fat 1.35 grams

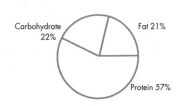

Carbohydrate 22%
Fat 21%
Protein 57%

* If you are making dumplings in the pot with the chicken, omit the cornstarch and add water if the gravy becomes too thick.

Buffalo Drumsticks

This is the leg version of the old wing standby. But for some reason these are named after a totally different—in every way, shape, and form—animal. Don't ask me why.

In case you've never chowed down on a buffalo anything, let me warn you that these legs are spicy, hot, and fabulous (kinda like mine).

Dip 'em in your favorite low-fat ranch dressing.

Appetizer 'em.

Late-night snack 'em.

And enjoy 'em.

½ cup Tabasco
2 tbsp rice vinegar
½ cup chicken broth
2 tbsp Molly McButter or Butter Buds
20 chicken legs, with skin removed
    Nonstick spray

Preheat oven to 450 degrees.

Combine Tabasco, vinegar, broth, and Molly McButter over low heat about 10 minutes. Remove from heat.

Place legs on cookie sheet sprayed with nonstick spray. Cook legs until brown, about 25 minutes. Pour sauce on top and cook 10 minutes more.

Serve with nonfat ranch dressing, green onions, celery sticks, and carrot sticks.

Nutritional:

Serving Size 5 legs
Servings per Recipe 4
Calories 397
Total Fat 12.65 grams
Saturated Fat 3.35 grams

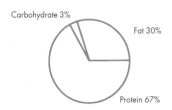

Carbohydrate 3%
Fat 30%
Protein 67%

Mediterranean Chicken

"Mediterranean"?

Sure, from the Mediterranean coast of Florida.

Chicken breast cooked in a light sauce with mushrooms, zucchini, red peppers, and onions: How good do you think this is going to taste? Delicate flavors for a nice light dinner, served over white or brown rice . . . just what your breast needs (chicken breast, of course).

1 medium onion, finely chopped
2 cloves garlic, sliced
6 boneless, skinless chicken breasts
1½ cups chicken broth
3 tbsp rice vinegar
¼ lb mushrooms, sliced
2 small zucchini, cut into ¼-inch cubes
1 red or green pepper, cut into thin strips
2 tsp Mrs. Dash garlic herb mix
¼ cup chopped parsley
  Salt to taste

Sweat onion and garlic until translucent. Add vegetables and cook briefly, about 2 minutes (vegetables should still be crisp). Remove from pan. Add chicken and cook over high heat until browned on both sides. Add broth and vinegar. Cook over high heat about 2 minutes, scraping pan. Add vegetables and spice mixture. Cook until chicken is cooked through, about 3 minutes. Serve over brown rice or pasta. Sprinkle with parsley and salt to taste.

Nutritional:

Serving Size 10 ounces
Servings per Recipe 6
Calories 191
Total Fat 3.25 grams
Saturated Fat 0.88 gram

Fat 15%
Protein 66%
Carbohydrate 19%

Tropical Chicken

Right from the Big Island.
Brought to the mainland by Susan Powter.

Hawaiian Chicken
Luau Lullaby
Tropical Taste in a Breast (tell your husband that's what you're making for dinner, and I doubt he'll ask you if it's low fat!!)

It's light.
It's sweet.
It gets four stars from all my taste testers.

Fab Ideas

Warm this baby up (leftover dream), throw in some raisins, stuff it in a warm piece of pita, and you've got Island Burrito.

Go crazy with some peach chutney, and you've got an Island Burrito with a Taste of India.

No matter what you do with your Tropical Chicken, you're gonna end up with a very pretty one-dish meal that's quick and easy (just like the girls with the bad reps in high school).

(Please! How stupid was that? The guys were slapped on the back and congratulated for every sexual act they could manage, and the girls were judged and juried on the spot. Unbelievable and amazing that this comes up in the middle of a chicken recipe. Oh, well, it's a democratic, freedom-of-speech, all-American kind of thing.)

Nonstick spray
6 skinless chicken breasts
1½ cups long-grain white rice
4 garlic cloves, minced
1 cup defatted chicken broth
1 cup orange juice
2 tsp ground ginger
2 tbsp ketchup
2 tbsp honey
3 tbsp rice vinegar
1 tbsp light soy or tamari sauce
1 20-oz (2½ cups) can pineapple chunks (packed in their own juice); drain juice, reserving 1 cup
Scallions for garnish

In a deep skillet sprayed with nonstick spray, brown chicken over high heat about 3 minutes on each side. Set aside on a plate. Add rice and garlic to pan and cook until rice is translucent. Place chicken over rice and add all the other ingredients, including pineapple juice. Bring to a boil and turn heat to low. Simmer, covered, until rice is cooked, about 30 minutes. Sprinkle scallions on top and serve.

Nutritional:

Serving Size 12 ounces
Servings per Recipe 6
Calories 426
Total Fat 3.45 grams
Saturated Fat 0.926 gram

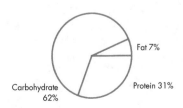

Fat 7%

Protein 31%

Carbohydrate 62%

Chicken à la King

We've got a king. THE KING. Chicken à la Elvis . . .

Let's just rename this dish. Whether it's American or not, we have to include it, it's so good—good as in 15 grams of fat less than your favorite basic version of Chicken à la King (what is the basic version, anyway?).

This is a good meal when you're in the mood for something not too spicy but chickeny and filling. Something that reminds you of ordering in. Something that conjures up images of plastic food in a display case.

Food for Thought

An à la Elvis suggestion: Try him over toast the next day with a salad and some saltines.

4 tbsp flour
1½ cups defatted chicken broth
1 cup cubed cooked chicken breast meat
1 cup sweated mushrooms
¼ cup chopped pimento or sweated red bell pepper
1 tsp Nature's Seasonings
1 tsp dry sherry (optional)
1 tbsp chopped parsley

Brown flour in a skillet sprayed with oil until very pale golden color. Add broth, stirring with a wire whisk until smooth. Add chicken, mushrooms, pimento, seasonings, and sherry and heat through. Serve over cooked noodles or rice. Sprinkle with parsley.

Nutritional:

Serving Size 10 ounces
Servings per Recipe 2
Calories 166
Total Fat 1.86 grams
Saturated Fat 0.475 gram

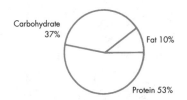

Carbohydrate 37%
Fat 10%
Protein 53%

Garlic Sauce Chicken

If you aren't madly in love with garlic, don't even bother with this recipe. Skip it and move on because we're talking GARLIC (as in one whole cup of fresh). This chicken doesn't have a chance but to end up garlicky.

If you couldn't care less what your breath smells like for the next month or two, try this over Confetti Rice (see page 196). Yellow from the corn, green from the peas and zucchini, and red from the purple onions (what the hell, let's ensure breath problems) make this a beautiful dish for all garlic lovers everywhere.

6 skinless chicken breasts
3 tbsp rice vinegar
1½ cups defatted chicken broth
1 cup whole peeled garlic cloves
1 tsp Spike seasoning
2 tbsp minced parsley

Preheat oven to 400 degrees.

Brown chicken breasts in a nonstick skillet. Remove chicken and add rice vinegar and chicken broth to pan. Cook over high heat for 2 minutes.

Put garlic cloves in a shallow baking dish (11 by 13 inches). Place chicken on top and pour sauce over. Sprinkle with Spike seasoning.

Bake for 30 minutes. Place chicken over cooled Confetti Rice in a serving dish. Mash garlic in the sauce, pour over top, and sprinkle with minced parsley.

Nutritional:

Serving Size 6 ounces
Servings per Recipe 6
Calories 171
Total Fat 2.98 grams
Saturated Fat 0.834 gram

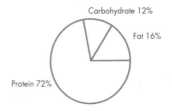

Carbohydrate 12%
Fat 16%
Protein 72%

Sesame Ginger Chicken with Brown Rice

Here's a recipe that you need to cook and eat—no lingering around the fridge and eating the next day for this dish because it's best when fresh. And since it's as easy as it gets, that's not gonna be a problem.

Quick, fresh, and fancy: American Oriental!

Maybe we've borrowed from the East, the mandarin oranges, the water chestnuts, the ginger, and the sesame seeds (don't we harvest sesame seeds on our farms? Come to think of it, where do those little seedlings come from???), but hey, we've added *American* orange juice—as all-American as you can get. And my first thought about this dish is what the hell would it be without the orange juice? So let's consider it American.

*P*sssst . . .

If you want to impress your organic friends, replace the white rice with brown. Simple substitution, and you're instantly very, very hip.

6 boneless, skinless chicken breasts
½ cup orange juice
3 tbsp tamari or light soy sauce
6 tbsp rice vinegar
3 tbsp honey
1 tsp *dark* sesame oil (yes, it makes a difference)
½ tsp dried ground ginger
¼ tsp crushed red pepper
1 tbsp sesame seeds
1 11-oz can mandarin oranges packed in own juice or light
   syrup, drained and with juice reserved
1 red bell pepper, cut into thin strips
½ cup finely chopped celery
½ cup finely chopped green onions
1 8-oz can water chestnuts, drained and sliced
½ lb Chinese (snow) peas or frozen peas
4 cups shredded napa cabbage (Chinese)
6 cups cooked brown rice

Over high heat in a large nonstick skillet sprayed with canola oil, brown chicken breasts about 4 minutes on each side. Remove chicken and slice into ½-inch strips.

Add orange juice, tamari, vinegar, honey, sesame oil, ginger, and red pepper to pan. Cook over high heat for about 2 minutes.

Return chicken to pan and cook 2 minutes more, or until the chicken is thoroughly cooked. Toss vegetables, except cabbage, with the chicken. Place cabbage on a platter, mound rice on top, and pour chicken mixture over all.

Nutritional:

Serving Size 18½ ounces
Servings per Recipe 6
Calories 479
Total Fat 7.03 grams
Saturated Fat 1.5 grams

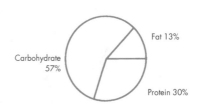

Fat 13%
Carbohydrate 57%
Protein 30%

Pepper Chicken

Pretty fancy, wouldn't you say? Chicken breast covered in fresh ground pepper and spices and cooked to perfection in a thin sauce with a little white wine added . . . Fancy Schmancy without doing a thing.

If you wanna go further with Fancy, take it to the edge of Schmancy, jump right into gourmet living, just add some Confetti Rice (see page 196) and Spinach Salad (see page 44). If that meal doesn't give you an attitude, nothing will.

Maybe this is the meal I should serve when I have the judge and his/her whole family over for dinner to help my citizenship request. Too much? Just enough?

½ tsp salt
1 tsp cracked pepper
1 tsp Mrs. Dash onion herb mix
4 boneless, skinless chicken breast halves
   Oil for spray
⅓ cup white wine
½ cup defatted chicken broth
½ cup nonfat sour cream

Combine salt, pepper, and Mrs. Dash. Sprinkle over and press pepper mixture into both sides of chicken. In a nonstick pan sprayed with oil, brown chicken on both sides over medium-high heat. Add wine and chicken broth and cook down until reduced by half, making sure chicken is cooked through. Remove chicken to a plate. Add sour cream to pan, combining well, and pour over chicken.

Nutritional:

Serving Size 7 ounces
Servings per Recipe 4
Calories 166
Total Fat 1.5 grams
Saturated Fat 0.394 gram

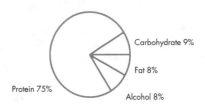

Carbohydrate 9%

Fat 8%

Protein 75%

Alcohol 8%

Philly Turkey Sandwich

Liberty bell.

Philly steak sandwich.

Part of the heart and soul of America, DONE.

Low-fat turkey, nonfat cheese, loaded with mushrooms and onions, broiled up, served on a French roll. Hearty, hot, and filling—who's gonna know this is low-fat?

Give this to the beef-eating people in your life and let 'em go to town!

Watch out: It's big, it's messy.

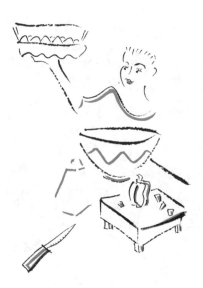

Nonstick spray
1 red onion, thinly sliced
6 oz mushrooms, sliced (optional)
¼ cup chicken broth
6 oz fat-free smoked turkey, thinly sliced (6–8 slices)
2 French rolls, split in half lengthwise
1 cup grated nonfat Monterey Jack or mozzarella cheese

Spray a sauté pan with nonstick spray. Fry onion over medium-high heat until brown. If using mushrooms, add to onions. Deglaze pan with ⅛ cup chicken broth. Remove onions and mushrooms and set aside.

In same pan, fry meat for about 3 minutes. Add remaining chicken broth.

Divide meat between two split French rolls. Place onions on top, cheese on top of onions. Place under broiler to melt cheese.

Serve with Dijon mustard and nonfat mayonnaise.

Nutritional:

Serving Size 24 ounces
Servings per Recipe 2
Calories 352
Total Fat 4.13 grams
Saturated Fat 0.366 gram

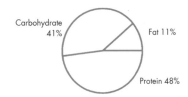

Carbohydrate 41%
Fat 11%
Protein 48%

Turkey Piccata

Gourmet without the fuss.

Fancy but easy.

A great topping for rice.

Invite everyone over and feed them something that will leave them talking about what a great cook you are.

About what you did with turkey.

About how health conscious you are.

About you.

You.

You.

You and your Turkey Piccata!

Nonstick spray
4 slices turkey breast, 1/4-inch thick
1/4 cup lemon juice
1/4 cup white wine
1/2 cup chicken broth
2 tbsp capers
1/2 tsp pepper
Salt to taste
1 tbsp finely chopped parsley

Heat a nonstick skillet sprayed with nonstick spray. Add turkey slices and brown on both sides. Remove to a plate. Add juice, wine, broth, and capers to the skillet. Cook over high heat a couple of minutes. Pour sauce over turkey and sprinkle with pepper, salt, and parsley. Serve with rice.

Nutritional:

Serving Size 6.2 ounces
Servings per Recipe 4
Calories 144
Total Fat 1.66 grams
Saturated Fat 0.432 gram

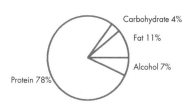

Carbohydrate 4%

Fat 11%

Alcohol 7%

Protein 78%

Chili Cornbread Pie

Chili Cornbread Pie . . .

This is a football kind of hearty—manly, very, very manly. I don't care what credit South American countries want to take for chili, we've had it for centuries. And if living together for seven years constitutes common-law marriage in some states, then consider chili the common-law food of the United States. It's ours.

It would be hard to make your chili pie any tastier, but you can make it healthier just by adding stone-ground cornmeal. It's grainier and richer; it will give you a crustier crust and a more nutritious meal.

Food for Thought

Great breakfast. This is one of those "better the second day" kind of meals. You have a couple of choices if you want to have a Chili Cornbread Pie breakfast. You can hold the football party over for a day or two—or boot the boys and have your Chili Cornbread Pie breakfast alone.

How's this: Egg white omelet with Chili Cornbread Pie on the side. Add a little salsa (my premenstrual dream). Well? Read the newspaper, make love to someone you love, and eat your Chili Cornbread Pie breakfast. If that isn't the perfect Sunday morning . . . And then . . . nap time!

Wake up and do it all again.

Am I talking a fabulous morning or what? Nobody ever did anything like this with a basic chili pie!

1 lb ground extra-lean turkey
1 cup chopped onion
$^1/_2$ cup chopped red bell pepper
2 cloves garlic, chopped fine
1 15-oz can black beans, drained and rinsed
1 15-oz can tomato sauce
1 28-oz can cut tomatoes
1 4-oz can whole green chilis, chopped coarsely

4 tbsp chili seasonings OR
2 tbsp chili powder
1 tsp cumin
1 tbsp onion powder
½ tsp garlic powder
½ tsp salt

Preheat oven to 400 degrees.

Brown turkey in a nonstick frying pan. Add onion and peppers and cook until limp. Drain well and place in a soup pot.

Add remaining ingredients, bring to a boil, and place in a large ovenproof dish.

Cover chili mixture with Cornbread batter (see page 210) and bake at 400 degrees until browned on top.

Serve with Nonfat Sour Cream Cilantro Sauce (see page 264).

Nutritional:

Serving Size 10 ounces
Servings per Recipe 8
Calories 142
Total Fat 1.5 grams
Saturated Fat 0.466 gram

Fat 9%

Carbohydrate 51%

Protein 40%

117

Sloppy Joes

Grab your partner,
   do-si-do.
   La, la, la,
   and grab a sloppy Joe. (Better stay away from songwriting, but you get the point.)
   Think elementary school. Cafeteria line. Once a week.
   And what does your brain start screaming?
   SLOPPY JOE!
   Can you have a sloppy Joe without fries? Nooooo.
   So what have we done for you?
   Check out page 178.
   Put 'em together and enjoy.

1 large red onion, chopped
1 large red bell pepper, chopped
2 cloves garlic, minced
1½ lb white meat ground turkey
1 12-oz bottle chili sauce
2 tbsp Worcestershire sauce
½ tsp Tabasco
2 tbsp rice vinegar

In a nonstick pan, cook onion, pepper, and garlic over medium heat for 5 minutes. Set aside in a bowl.

Put turkey in a pan, crumble into chunks, and cook until no longer pink.

Return vegetables to pan, add remaining ingredients except vinegar, and simmer for 10 minutes. Add vinegar and serve over split rolls.

Nutritional:

Serving Size 7½ ounces
Servings per Recipe 6
Calories 196
Total Fat 1.74 grams
Saturated Fat 2.93 grams

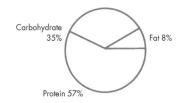

Carbohydrate 35%
Fat 8%
Protein 57%

Meatloaf

As American as . . . .

But let's face it, meatloaf has always been kind of a "gaggy" food. With all due respect to the loaf made of meat, it's common! On the table once a week for forever.

Meatloaf needs a bit of an overhaul, and who better to do it than Yankee Doodle Sue? With the enthusiasm of a born-again anything, I've reinvented the MEATLOAF. Thank you.

I can't tell you how good this new and improved, lower-fat MEATLOAF is. You could enter this sucker into any state fair contest in the country—even if it's the baking contest. Let everyone else bring their best muffins and pies. Rile 'em up a bit by putting your MEATLOAF down on the counter. Stick a HUGE American flag through the center. That'll get 'em going. Oh, the judges will be mad at first, but once they get a taste of this low-fat, meatier-than-meaty loaf, they'll forgive your lack of judgment and you'll win.

Crafty Cooking Suggestions: Double the recipe and make two loaves at once. Freeze one and pull it out when you need it. How crafty is that?

I suppose you could get even craftier and get some of that goop in tubes that you decorate cakes with and draw an American flag on the top if you like . . . I told you I wasn't good at the crafty stuff.

Fancy Schmancy

You're laughing, aren't ya? You don't think there is such a thing as meatloaf getting fancy?

How about pâté. Yeah, pâté. As in about as fancy as you can get. People will rave about your pâté, your *meatloaf* pâté. Don't you love that?

Take your loaf—that sounds appealing—and spread it over your favorite low-fat cracker—not the whole loaf, just a bit. Smear, smear, smear it over, add a little salt, and some parsley if you really want to go overboard . . .

Cooking spray
3/4 lb lean ground beef (10 percent fat)
1 cup chopped onion
1 cup chopped carrots
1 cup chopped celery
2 tsp chopped garlic
3 egg whites
1/2 cup bread crumbs
1/4 cup ketchup
1/4 cup beef bouillon
1 tsp basil
1/2 tsp oregano
1 tsp salt
1/2 tsp pepper
1 cup finely chopped potatoes
1/4 cup chopped parsley

Preheat oven to 350 degrees.

Sauté onion, carrots, and celery in a nonstick pan with a little cooking spray until soft. Set aside until cool. Add all other ingredients to chopped meat.

Form mixture into a loaf about 4 inches high and place on lightly oiled baking pan (use light oil spray). Cover with aluminum foil.

Bake for 30 minutes. Remove foil and bake 30 minutes more.

Let meatloaf rest 10 minutes, then slice and serve with your favorite sauce or gravy.

Nutritional:

Serving Size 6 ounces
Servings per Recipe 6
Calories 155
Total Fat 4.89 grams
Saturated Fat 1.86 grams

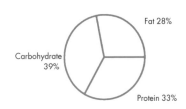

Fat 28%
Carbohydrate 39%
Protein 33%

All-American,
All-Purpose Meatballs

What can't you do with meatballs?

Make them big for a bowl of spaghetti.

Make them small, stick in a toothpick, and we're talking perfect appetizer.

Leftover meatballs in a hoagie with tomato sauce and Parmesan cheese—what could be better?

Meatballs with Mushroom Onion Gravy (page 274) over Down-home Mashed Potatoes (page 174), rice, or pasta for a fabulous hearty dinner.

There's only one thing that you can't do with a meatball: make it American. Even I can't stretch it that far. The settlers eating spaghetti and meatballs by the campfire? Thanksgiving turkey and spaghetti and meatballs? I don't think so. But just this once, let's overlook it because you're gonna want this recipe. So what if it's a not-so-American recipe in an all-American cookbook. Who's looking so closely?

½ cup minced onion
   Nonstick spray
3 egg whites, beaten
4 tbsp finely chopped parsley
1½ tsp Spike seasoning
½ tsp thyme
½ tsp marjoram
½ tsp white pepper
1½ lb extra-lean ground turkey
2 cups fresh bread crumbs
2 tbsp flour
2 cups chicken broth
1 tbsp dry sherry

Sauté onion in pan sprayed with nonstick spray.

Combine egg whites with parsley, spices, and onion. Add turkey and stir. Work in bread crumbs, kneading by hand if necessary. Shape into 1½-inch balls. Brown meatballs in nonstick skillet.

Remove from pan, add flour, brown lightly, and add chicken broth and sherry. Return meatballs to pan and simmer 10 minutes.

Makes 20 half-inch meatballs.

Nutritional:

Serving Size 6 ounces
Servings per Recipe 8
Calories 127
Total Fat 1.29 grams
Saturated Fat 0.602 gram

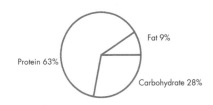

Fat 9%

Protein 63%

Carbohydrate 28%

Beef Stew

Raise the American flag when you make this recipe.

We're talking all-American on this beef stew. Nothing herb-y about it. A classic *Leave It to Beaver*, Donna Reed, T-bird, cigarette in the sleeve, poodle skirt kind of beef stew. The way beef stew was meant to be. You gotta double this because it freezes like a champ.

Defrost, Warm Up, Think About This:

Wrap it in a tortilla.
Stuff it in an omelet.
Put it over rice.
Set it on toast.

3/4 lb beef round, cut into cubes
1 tsp salt
1/2 tsp pepper
1 tbsp vegetable oil
2 1/4 cups chopped onion
2 garlic cloves, minced
1/2 tsp marjoram
1 bay leaf
1/2 tsp thyme
1/2 cup red wine
1 lb red potatoes, peeled and cut into 1-inch chunks
2 large carrots, sliced into 1/4-inch rounds
1/2 lb green beans, cut into 1 1/2-inch pieces
2 tbsp chopped parsley for garnish

Season beef with salt and pepper.

Heat oil in a casserole and sauté beef until lightly browned. Remove and set aside.

Add onion to pan and cook 5–7 minutes, until it begins to brown. Add garlic and cook 1 minute more.

Return beef and any juices to pan, add marjoram, bay leaf, thyme, wine, and 2½ cups water, or to cover. Lower heat and cook for 1 hour.

Add potatoes and carrots, and cook for 35 minutes. Add beans and simmer until beef and vegetables are tender, about 10 minutes. Check potatoes to be sure they are soft.

Remove 1 cup of potatoes, mash with a fork, and return to casserole to thicken gravy. Heat through. Adjust seasonings and serve garnished with chopped parsley.

Nutritional:

Serving Size 14 ounces
Servings per Recipe 4
Calories 370
Total Fat 10.3 grams
Saturated Fat 2.57 grams

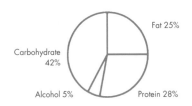

Fat 25%
Carbohydrate 42%
Alcohol 5%
Protein 28%

Low-fat Patty Melt

Never thought you'd have a hot deli sandwich again, did ya?

Serve this up with Potato Wedges (see page 182) or fries, coleslaw, potato salad, and pickles, and tell me if anyone complains about saving up to 15 grams of fat by eating this instead of the high-high-fat versions of the past.

COME ON AMERICA, LET'S EAT!

AND ENJOY OUR FOOD AGAIN

AND NOT DIE OF HEART DISEASE AND OBESITY. . . .

(Your honor)

1 lb extra-lean ground turkey
1 cup cooked rice
2 tsp Nature's Seasonings
1 tsp Mrs. Dash onion herb mix
    Nonstick spray
1 red onion, thinly sliced
¼ cup chicken broth
2 cups grated nonfat mozzarella cheese
8 slices thick rye bread
    Nonfat mayonnaise

Combine turkey, rice, 1 teaspoon of Nature's Seasonings, and onion herb mix. Shape into patties about 4 inches in diameter and ½ to ¾ inch thick.

Spray a pan with nonstick spray. Fry onion over high heat, until limp and brown, adding the remaining teaspoon of Nature's Seasonings.

Add chicken broth to release the browned bits in the pan. Remove from pan and set aside.

In the same pan, fry the turkey patties over medium-high heat. Brown 5 minutes on each side, or until thoroughly cooked. During the last 2 minutes put ½ cup of cheese on each patty. Cover pan and cook until cheese melts.

Spread both sides of rye bread with nonfat mayonnaise. Fry the bread in a nonstick skillet on one side. Put grilled onions on top of each patty. Put patty on the uncooked side of the bread, covering with the other slice of bread.

Serve with Dijon mustard or creamy horseradish sauce. Serve potato salad or coleslaw on the side.

Nutritional:

Serving Size 11 ounces
Servings per Recipe 4
Calories 427
Total Fat 3.30 grams
Saturated Fat 1.25 grams

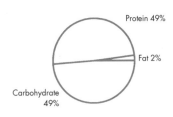

Protein 49%

Fat 2%

Carbohydrate 49%

All-American Burger

Raise the flag, play "The Star-Spangled Banner," and get out the war medals because as far back as anyone can remember this country was cooking up hamburger.

Serve this baby with all your favorite toppings:
  - lettuce
  - tomato
  - low-fat mayo
  - mustard
  - catsup
  - nonfat cheese melted on.

Grill some onions and mushrooms, and put 'em on.

Get out your favorite salsa (check the label for oil) and pile on the jalapeños.

Recite the pledge of allegiance and EAT.

¼ lb extra-lean ground turkey
½ tsp onion powder
½ tsp garlic powder
¼ tsp Nature's Seasonings
 1 tsp finely chopped parsley
⅓ cup chicken broth
 1 low-fat or nonfat hamburger bun

Combine turkey, onion powder, garlic powder, Nature's Seasonings, and parsley. Form into a patty the same size as the bun. Heat a skillet sprayed with nonstick spray. Place patty in the pan and brown on both sides, about 4 minutes per side. Pour broth into pan and cook until broth is almost gone. Place on bun and garnish with lettuce, tomato, pickle, nonfat mayonnaise, and Dijon mustard if desired. Serve with fries.

Nutritional:

Serving Size 8½ ounces
Servings per Recipe 1
Calories 269
Total Fat 3.65 grams
Saturated Fat 1.44 grams

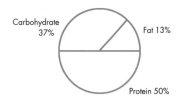

Carbohydrate 37%
Fat 13%
Protein 50%

Fried Pork Chops with Gravy

Here's a meal that millions of people eat, a meal that desperately needs some defatting, with all due respect to the Deep South.

This is a "slow, lazy afternoon in the kitchen" kind of dish. It takes a good forty-five minutes to make, but it's great-tasting for tomorrow—say, after-church dinner—so cook it up today, reheat it tomorrow, and say a prayer for me.

4 ½-inch-thick center-cut loin pork chops, with fat trimmed
½ tsp salt
½ tsp pepper
½ lb mushrooms, sliced
1 medium onion, sliced
¾ cup defatted chicken broth
2 tbsp tomato sauce
1 tsp onion powder
½ tsp garlic powder
1 tbsp Dijon mustard
2 tbsp sour cream
2 tbsp chopped parsley

Sprinkle chops with salt and pepper. Place in a nonstick skillet and brown over high heat about 3 minutes on each side. Remove from skillet.

Place mushrooms and onion in pan and cook on medium-high for 5 minutes. Add broth, tomato sauce, onion and garlic powders, and mustard to pan. Cook for 1 minute.

Return chops to pan and cook, covered, for 10 minutes longer, or until chops are thoroughly cooked. Place chops on a plate. Stir sour cream into sauce in pan and then pour over chops. Sprinkle with parsley and serve over bowtie noodles.

Nutritional:

Serving Size 7 ounces
Servings per Recipe 4
Calories 156
Total Fat 5.34 grams
Saturated Fat 1.9 grams

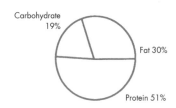

Carbohydrate 19%

Fat 30%

Protein 51%

Tuna Noodle Casserole

PTA.

Pot Luck City.

Having a bunch of friends over . . .

A throw-together meal like you've never . . .

Fancy Schmancy

Fancy this up by using fresh cooked tuna and serve it with seasonal fresh steamed veggies.

You're ready to ring the dinner bell.

½ cup sliced celery
½ lb fresh mushrooms, sliced
1 tsp celery salt
8 ounces noodles, cooked according to package directions
2 6-oz cans water-packed tuna, well drained
1½ cups nonfat sour cream
¾ cup nonfat milk
1 tsp Mrs. Dash onion herb mixture
½ tsp white pepper
Nonstick butter-flavored spray
¼ cup nonfat Parmesan cheese
¼ cup dry bread crumbs
¼ cup chopped parsley

Preheat oven to 350 degrees.

Sweat celery and mushrooms in a nonstick pan and sprinkle with salt. Combine with noodles, tuna, sour cream, herb mixture, and pepper. Turn into a 2-quart casserole sprayed with nonstick spray.

Mix together Parmesan, bread crumbs, and parsley. Sprinkle over top of casserole and spray with nonstick spray.

Bake, uncovered, for 35–40 minutes.

Nutritional:

Serving Size 9 ounces
Servings per Recipe 6
Calories 222
Total Fat 1.28 grams
Saturated Fat 0.310 gram

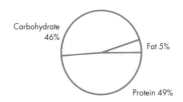

Carbohydrate 46%
Fat 5%
Protein 49%

Shrimp Creole

Swamp boy.

Hot stuff.

Spice over rice.

Onions, garlic, tomatoes, parsley, and hot spices combined. We're talking Creole, Creole, Creole.

Shrimp being America's favorite shellfish (did you know that?) and "Creole" anything being damn good makes this one of America's new favorite dishes.

2 medium onions, chopped
3 cloves garlic, minced
2 stalks celery, chopped
1 14½-oz can chicken or vegetable broth
1 tbsp lemon juice
1 28-oz can crushed or chopped tomatoes
1 bay leaf
3 drops Louisiana hot sauce (Tabasco)
1 tsp Mrs. Dash onion and herb seasoning
1 tsp Mrs. Dash garlic and herb seasoning
¼ tsp celery salt
¼ tsp white pepper
1 tsp Spike seasoning
1½ lb uncooked shelled shrimp

In a medium-size pot or Dutch oven, sweat onions, garlic, and celery until soft and browned.

Add broth and lemon juice. Then add tomatoes and spices. Simmer for at least 1 hour.

Add shrimp and simmer until shrimp are pink and opaque (about 3 to 5 minutes).

Remove bay leaf before serving. Sprinkle with chopped parsley.

$\mathcal{F}$ab Idea

Add 2 cups sliced okra to pot after simmering for half an hour, and continue simmering for an additional half hour.

$\mathcal{N}utritional$:

Serving Size 8.8 ounces
Servings per Recipe 6
Calories 134
Total Fat 2.06 grams
Saturated Fat 0.322 gram

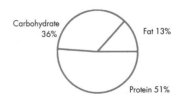

Carbohydrate 36%
Fat 13%
Protein 51%

Crunchy Fish Fillets

What we all grew up on, except now the fat is missing. These "kids' favorites" take minutes to throw together, are lower in fat and great tasting, and can be fancied up in a second. . . .

Serve them with Orange Cilantro Sauce, page 248.

Dressed down for the kids, use catsup!

Arthur Treacher should be shaking in his boots!

1 cup nonfat yogurt
2 egg whites, beaten
2 tsp Spike seasoning
4 fillets of orange roughy or other mild, firm-textured fish
2 cups seasoned bread crumbs

Preheat oven to 450 degrees.

Combine yogurt, egg whites and Spike. Thoroughly coat each fillet with this mixture and then dip in bread crumbs, pressing crumbs into fish. Put in a shallow baking pan that has been sprayed with nonstick spray. Bake at 450 degrees for about 10 minutes, or until brown on top and crispy.

Nutritional:

Serving Size 8.7 ounces
Servings per Recipe 4
Calories 263
Total Fat 2.07 grams
Saturated Fat 0.295 gram

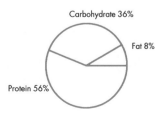

Carbohydrate 36%
Fat 8%
Protein 56%

Swordfish Kabobs

Come on, replace the meat on your usual kabobs (like kabobs are a normal part of your life) with swordfish marinated in a zingy, tangy sauce of ginger, lime, rice vinegar, and tamari and go to town.

Grill it, broil it, or bake it and serve it over rice. The American kabob will never be the same again.

1 lb swordfish, cut into 2-inch cubes
12 cherry tomatoes
2 onions, quartered
1 red bell pepper, cut into 2-inch pieces
1 green bell pepper, cut into 2-inch pieces
1 zucchini, sliced into ½-inch-thick slices
1 cup Ginger Garlic Soy Lime Dressing (see page 78)

Put swordfish and vegetables onto skewers, alternating each, and place in a shallow pan. Pour Ginger Garlic Soy Lime Dressing over fish and vegetables, turning the skewers every 15 minutes for an hour. Grill over coals, or spray cookie sheet with nonstick spray and broil or bake until browned at 500 degrees. Serve over rice.

Nutritional:

Serving Size 11.8 ounces
Servings per Recipe 4
Calories 213
Total Fat 5.42 grams
Saturated Fat 1.37 grams

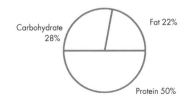

Carbohydrate 28%
Fat 22%
Protein 50%

Chop Suey or Chow Mein

Chop suey—all-American! Maybe not when served over rice, but add some noodles and, bingo, you're talking American chop suey.

There's only one little problem with this dish. Lots o' chopping!!! Maybe we should call it chop-a-lot suey.

1 tsp canola oil
1 cup celery, chopped into 1/4-inch slices
1 cup green onions, sliced into 1-inch pieces
1 cup shiitake (Chinese) mushrooms, sliced 1/4 inch thick (if using dried, soak in warm water 15 minutes, until soft. Cut off tough stems)
1 red bell pepper, seeded and cut into 1/4-inch strips
2 cloves garlic, chopped
1 tbsp fresh peeled and chopped ginger, or 1 tsp dried ginger
1 carrot, peeled and cut into 1/4-inch-thick strips 1 inch long
1 can water chestnuts, sliced
1 1/2 cups bean sprouts, fresh preferred
1/4 lb Chinese pea pods, stems and tips removed (if unavailable, use 1 cup frozen peas)
2 cups vegetable broth
4 tbsp soy sauce or tamari
4 tbsp dry sherry
1/2 tsp chili oil (optional)
2 tbsp rice vinegar
2 tbsp cornstarch
2 tbsp water
6 cups cooked rice, or 1 lb thin spaghetti noodles, cooked in broth

In a large pan over high heat, sauté all vegetables in canola oil, except sprouts and pea pods, for 4 minutes. Add pea pods, sprouts, broth, soy sauce, chili oil, if using, and rice vinegar. Combine cornstarch and water, add to pan and stir thoroughly. Cook 3 minutes more. Serve over rice (chop suey) or cooked noodles (chow mein).

Nutritional: Chop Suey

Serving Size 17 ounces
Servings per Recipe 6
Calories 371
Total Fat 1.95 grams
Saturated Fat 0.274 gram

Fat 4%
Alcohol less than 1%
Protein 10%
Carbohydrate 85%

Nutritional: Chow Mein

Serving Size 20 ounces
Servings per Recipe 6
Calories 652
Total Fat 3.15 grams
Saturated Fat 0.445 gram

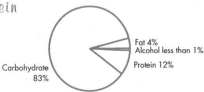

Fat 4%
Alcohol less than 1%
Protein 12%
Carbohydrate 83%

Soy Ginger Noodles

Delicious little traditional number.

Soy beans, we grow them.

Ginger, nobody knows where that really comes from, and . . .

Noodles are definitely ours.

This is the ramen noodley stuff that everyone loves except it doesn't have that charming pre-packaged taste.

Fab Ideas

Serve this over shredded Chinese cabbage.

Add some cooked shrimp or leftover grilled chicken and it's a meal and a half.

1 12-oz package angel hair pasta, broken in half and cooked
  per package directions
1 lb asparagus, cut into 2-inch pieces and steamed 3 minutes
3 green onions, with some green tops, chopped
½ red bell pepper cut into thin strips
1 yellow squash, shredded
6 shiitake mushrooms, sliced and sautéed 5 minutes*
1 11-oz can mandarin oranges, drained
1 cup Ginger Garlic Soy Lime Dressing (see page 78)

Toss all ingredients together and refrigerate.

*If using dried mushrooms, soak them just covered in warm
water to cover for half an hour, until soft. Cut off woody stems
and slice.

Nutritional:

Serving Size 11.5 ounces
Servings per Recipe 6
Calories 234
Total Fat 1.36 grams
Saturated Fat 0.21 gram

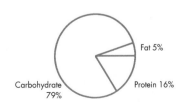

Fat 5%

Protein 16%

Carbohydrate
79%

Western Omelet

You gotta have your mushroom, onion, ham, cheese, spicy, great-tasting omelet on Sunday morning while you read your newspaper, and you don't want the 37 grams (and that's just for three eggs and a slice of cheese) of extra fat that you don't need attaching itself to your thighs. So what do you do?

P.S. from Me . . .

Take out the yolk and go to town. Eat this for breakfast, lunch, dinner, or a snack with Potato Wedges (see page 182) and Salsa (see page 252), and tell me that you need all that fat to get the taste!!!

4 egg whites, beaten
1 tbsp nonfat evaporated milk
1 tbsp chopped red onion
2 tbsp diced red bell pepper
3 mushrooms, sliced
2 tbsp diced nonfat turkey ham
½ tsp Nature's Seasonings or Spike seasoning
¼ cup grated nonfat cheese (any kind)
1 tbsp chopped parsley
2 tbsp nonfat sour cream

Mix egg whites and evaporated milk and set aside.

Sauté onion, pepper, mushrooms, and ham for 5 minutes in a saucepan. Set aside.

Wipe nonstick omelet pan with oil, leaving just a trace. Heat pan over medium-high heat. Pour egg whites in pan, tipping pan and lifting the sides of the egg whites with a spatula so uncooked whites runs underneath. When the omelet is just starting to set, sprinkle seasoning on top.

Add the vegetable-ham mixture and cheese. Fold omelet in half and slide onto plate.

Sprinkle with parsley and serve with sour cream on the side.

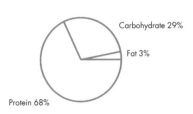

Nutritional:

Serving Size 11 ounces
Servings per Recipe 1
Calories 191
Total Fat 0.502 gram
Saturated Fat 0.105 gram

Carbohydrate 29%
Fat 3%
Protein 68%

Zucchini Cheese Pie

American Quiche!!!

The French aren't gonna like this much, but then again, the French don't like anything much.

(I just got back from Paris with my son. And no, they don't have *tooo* much of an attitude! I'm telling you the truth when I say that I kissed the ground we landed on back here—and that's coming from someone who is a wannabe American. Great food, pretty city, fab time with my son, but hey, hey, hey, let's bring that attitude down about a hundred notches.)

Warning on this one: If you don't like garlic, onions, jalapeños . . . If you are a bottom-line kind of gal . . .

DON'T TRY THIS DISH.

This is absolutely for the European wannabes. The glass-of-wine-in-the-evening-with-the-small-spinach-salad-on-the-side-and-slice-of-bread-eating folk. We are talking entertainment city with this little cheesy pie dish. You don't get a better brunch food. Have you got a brunch that sounds better than Zucchini Cheese Pie with fresh fruit salad and Potato Wedges (see page 182)?

Perfectly Sinful Suggestion from Me:

Do something special just for you. Lie to the world. Tell the husband, boyfriend, kids, family, friends that you have been called out of town or must visit someone who doesn't exist—do whatever you have to do to get the place to yourself.

Make a Zucchini Cheese Pie.

Take a bubble bath.

Slip into something beautiful (listen to me on this one; I'm right). Don't just dress up for everyone else, dress up for yourself.

Put on some of your favorite music. Light a candle.

Read your favorite book. Set a beautiful table for yourself . . .

Eat and enjoy.

1 tsp olive oil
½ cup chopped onion
2 tsp minced garlic
1 jalapeño, finely chopped (optional)
1½ lb zucchini, cut into ¼-inch circles
½ cup chopped red bell pepper
¼ tsp basil
1 tsp salt
½ tsp black pepper
1 egg
2 egg whites
1 cup nonfat cottage cheese
  Nonstick spray
1 tbsp grated Parmesan cheese

Preheat oven to 350 degrees.

Heat oil in a nonstick pan. Sauté onion, garlic, and jalapeño pepper until the onion is soft. Add 2 tablespoons of water if too dry. Add zucchini and red pepper, and continue cooking until zucchini is tender but still firm. Add seasonings and set aside.

Mix eggs and cottage cheese with a fork until well blended.

Spray a 10-inch pie plate with nonstick spray. Place vegetable mixture in bottom of pie plate. Cover with egg and cottage cheese mixture. Sprinkle Parmesan cheese on top.

Bake for 30 minutes, or until a knife inserted in the middle comes out clean.

Nutritional:

Serving Size 11 ounces
Servings per Recipe 4
Calories 122
Total Fat 3.18 grams
Saturated Fat 0.903 gram

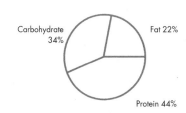

Carbohydrate 34%
Fat 22%
Protein 44%

Perfect breakfast food. Not just as a side dish: Slice some tomato and have this on toast.

Eggs McLeaner Thighs

It takes five minutes to make and tastes better than any drive-thru McAnything could ever taste.

You can send the kids out the door with an Egg McLeaner wrapped up and ready to eat.

Make a bunch of these, wrap 'em in foil, and take them along to sports events.

They're just right for you while you're running all over town or to the office . . .

Low fat can't be convenient and taste great? I don't think so: You've got 'em both right here!

1 tbsp rice vinegar
1 English muffin, split and toasted
2 egg whites, poached together and drained
1 slice nonfat cheddar cheese
1 slice nonfat ham

Simmer 1 inch of water and vinegar in a shallow pan. Add egg whites. Poach until firm, then remove with a slotted spoon and drain on paper towels. Place egg, cheese, and ham on muffin. Put other muffin half on top and microwave for 1 minute.

Nutritional:

Serving Size 5½ ounces
Servings per Recipe 1
Calories 217
Total Fat 1.17 grams
Saturated Fat 0.141 gram

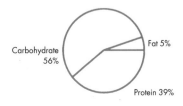

Carbohydrate 56%
Fat 5%
Protein 39%

Eggs Florentine

You want a challenge? Take a fancy schmancy egg dish that's about as high fat as you get (25 grams per serving—heart disease city), that has nothing to do with America (it's Florentine), make it low fat but still fabulous tasting, and connect the red, white, and blue.

It's a done deal. This as-fancy-as-you-get-for-breakfast dish is fabulous! Whip it up when you're in the mood to impress and enjoy it.

Suggestion from the Chef

This is a serve-and-eat dish. Can you imagine leftovers on this one?
YUUUUUUUKKKKK.

¼ cup chopped green onion
1 clove garlic, finely chopped
1 10-oz package frozen chopped leaf spinach, cooked and
squeezed dry
¼ cup vegetable broth
4 English muffins, split and toasted (keep warm in a 200-degree
oven)
Lemon Dijon Sauce (see page 262)
8 egg whites, poached
⅛ tsp cayenne pepper

Sauté onion and garlic in a skillet. Add spinach and broth and cook until the broth is absorbed. Spread each muffin half with Lemon Dijon Sauce. Put spinach on each muffin half. Place 1 poached egg white on top of spinach. Pour sauce over each egg, sprinkle with cayenne, and serve.

Poached Eggs

Water
2 tbsp rice vinegar
4 egg whites, in separate bowls

Bring 1 to 2 inches of water and rice vinegar to simmer in shallow 8-inch saute pan. Slide egg whites, one at a time, into water. Simmer until firm, then remove with a slotted spoon and drain on paper towels.

Nutritional:

Serving Size 8 ounces
Servings per Recipe 4
Calories 195
Total Fat 1.33 grams
Saturated Fat 0.185 gram

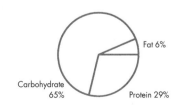

Fat 6%

Carbohydrate 65%

Protein 29%

*Boring, boring, boring. What's more
connected to diets than carrot sticks? How many
times can you make steamed vegetables before
you run for the ribeye? I'm with ya.
Understandable. That's why we got you some of
the best vegetable dishes in the land . . . this
beautiful land of yours that I'd like very much to
be a part of, your honor. Clear the slate on
vegetables until you've made some of these
recipes. You'll never look at a veggie the same
way again. From now on,*

> *This veggie is your veggie.*
> *This veggie is my veggie.*
> *From the purple mountains to the redwood
> forests.*
> *From the gulfstream waters to the . . .*

*I think I've taken this all-American theme too
far, what do you think?*

Vegetables

Sweet-and-Sour Cabbage

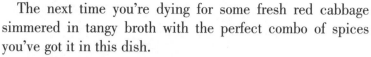

The next time you're dying for some fresh red cabbage simmered in tangy broth with the perfect combo of spices you've got it in this dish.

I'm telling you, not only is this Sweet-and-Sour Cabbage a perfect holiday dish (break the old cranberry sauce routine and throw some Sweet-and-Sour Cabbage on the holiday table), but it's the perfect side dish with a sweet-and-sour bite.

Great with Down-home Mashed Potatoes (see page 174) as a vegetarian meal.

Or serve it with grilled loin pork chops or any grilled meat or chicken.

Sweet, sour, *and* diversified.

6 cups shredded red cabbage
$1/4$ cup rice vinegar
$1/4$ cup water
1 tsp Nature's Seasonings
$3/4$ tsp caraway seeds
$1/4$ tsp pepper
2 slices bacon, cooked and crumbled (optional)

Combine all ingredients in a deep pan. Cook over medium heat for 15–20 minutes, or until cabbage is limp.

Nutritional (with bacon):

Serving Size 3.5 ounces
Servings per Recipe 6
Calories 35
Total Fat 0.9 gram
Saturated Fat 0.251 gram

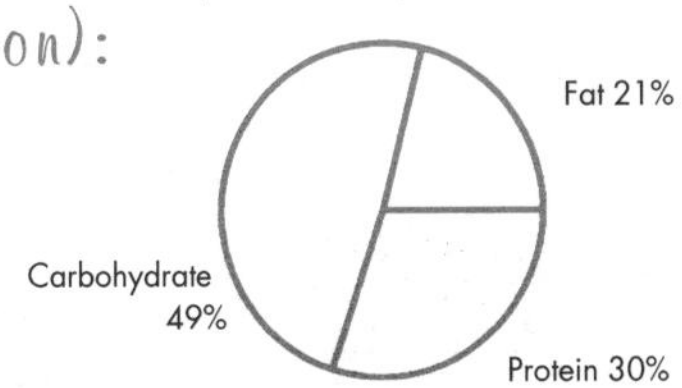

Fat 21%
Carbohydrate 49%
Protein 30%

Nutritional (without bacon):

Serving Size 3.2 ounces
Servings per Recipe 6
Calories 20
Total Fat 0.238 gram
Saturated Fat 0.029 gram

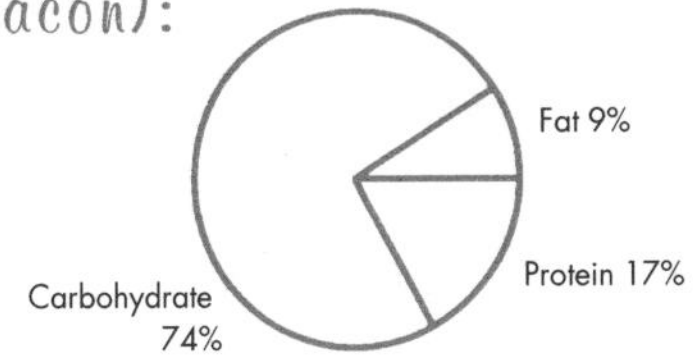

Fat 9%
Protein 17%
Carbohydrate 74%

Sweet-and-Sour Stuffed Cabbage

Cabbage has always had a bad reputation. Gas. Forced to eat it as a child. Smells terrible when you're cooking it. So I thought it was time to rejuvenate, to reinstate, to reestablish the reputation of the all-American cabbage—starting with Sweet-and-Sour (red, white, and blue) Stuffed Cabbage.

(We owe this to Cabbage Patch dolls. What was the deal with those things? Cabbage Patch dolls and Pet Rocks—I bought both!!!!)

This is a one-dish vegetarian complete meal.

Or, served with a salad and hot dinner rolls, it's a perfect complete meal that will, without a doubt, resurrect the cabbage, but hopefully not the Cabbage Patch doll!!!!

1 medium onion, chopped
1 clove garlic, minced
3 cups cooked rice (brown preferred)
2 tsp Spike seasoning
1/8 tsp cloves
2 egg whites, beaten
1 head cabbage, core removed, steamed until leaves can be
   pulled off easily
1 16-oz can chopped tomatoes
1/4 cup sugar
1/2 cup raisins (less if you don't love raisins)
6 tbsp rice vinegar

Sauté onion and garlic. Mix with rice, 1 teaspoon of Spike, cloves, and egg whites. Place 2 tablespoons in the center of a cabbage leaf. Fold the sides up and roll up. Place seam side down in an 11-by-13-inch baking dish. Prepare additional rolls—there will be a total of 10 to 12.

Mix tomatoes, raisins, the remaining teaspoon of Spike, sugar, and vinegar in a pot over low heat until sugar dissolves. Pour mixture over cabbage rolls. Bake at 375 degrees for 35 minutes.

Serve with nonfat sour cream on the side.

Nutritional:

Serving Size 14 ounces
Servings per Recipe 6
Calories 247
Total Fat 1.59 grams
Saturated Fat 0.289 gram

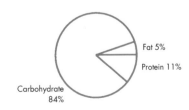

Fat 5%

Protein 11%

Carbohydrate
84%

Sugar-Glazed Carrots

Thanksgiving city . . .

A great way to get the kids to devour carrots . . .

Fresh sliced carrots cooked with brown sugar, orange juice, rice vinegar, and a little ginger, fabulously fancy but simple. I love this dish and have decided to enter it in the next State Fair Carrot Cooking Contest I enter. . . .

And there's a chance of that happening!!!

8 carrots, cut into ⅛-inch slices
¼ cup brown sugar
¼ cup orange juice
2 tbsp rice vinegar
⅛ tsp ginger
½ tsp Spike seasoning
1 tsp Butter Buds

Cook carrots for 8 minutes, or until crisp tender, then drain. Combine remaining ingredients with carrots and simmer 10 minutes more over low heat. Mix well so that carrots are completely coated with glaze.

Nutritional:

Serving Size 4 ounces
Servings per Recipe 6
Calories 71
Total Fat 0.208 gram
Saturated Fat 0.037 gram

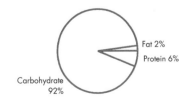

Fat 2%
Protein 6%
Carbohydrate 92%

Creamy Cauliflower

Grosssssss!

Nursing Home lunch?

I was with ya until I tasted this big head of cauliflower baked in a creamy, cheesy sauce, a delicious, delicious creamed cauliflower dish. Consider this one of the fanciest ways to serve a vegetable dish, a perfect side dish for any dinner, and the only way ever to eat cauliflower again.

$\mathcal{P}$ssssst . . .

Amazing suggestion. Creamed Cauliflower for breakfast! Swear. Try it over toast first thing in the morning. It's great.

1 head cauliflower, broken into florets
½ cup nonfat mayonnaise
¼ cup nonfat sour cream
2 tsp Dijon mustard
½ cup shredded nonfat cheddar cheese
½ tsp Nature's Seasonings
2 tbsp lemon juice
2 tbsp finely chopped parsley

Preheat oven to 375 degrees. Cook cauliflower for about 10 minutes, until just tender. Place in an 8 by 8-inch baking dish. Combine remaining ingredients and pour over cauliflower. Bake at 375 degrees for 10 minutes.

Nutritional:

Serving Size 4 ounces
Servings per Recipe 4
Calories 72
Total Fat 0.098 gram
Saturated Fat 0.016 gram

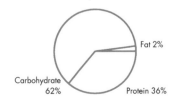

Fat 2%

Carbohydrate 62%

Protein 36%

Scalloped Corn and Potatoes

The best. The old way was tasty, sure, but how about that 40 percent calories from fat!!!

Wondering why you've gotten fatter over the years? Well, not anymore.

Sliced potatoes, corn, onions, and spices in a cheesy cream sauce baked in a casserole until bubbling hot with less fat coming right up.

½ cup finely chopped red onion
½ tsp salt
¼ tsp pepper
   pinch of cayenne
2 cups Basic Cream Sauce (see page 258)
3 medium potatoes, steamed until just tender, and sliced ¼ inch
   thick
1 10-oz box frozen corn
1 cup grated nonfat cheddar cheese
1 tbsp chopped parsley

Preheat oven to 375 degrees.

Sauté onion until soft. Add seasonings to Basic Cream Sauce. Layer potatoes, corn, and onion with cream sauce in a baking dish. Sprinkle with cheese and parsley. Bake in 375-degree oven for 20 minutes.

Nutritional:

Serving Size 7.7 ounces
Servings per Recipe 6
Calories 180
Total Fat 0.295 gram
Saturated Fat 0.119 gram

Fat 2%
Protein 25%
Carbohydrate 73%

Eggplant Parmigiana

Your first thought is Italian, right? You'd think with a name like parmigiana ... All because it's a dish you'll find in most Italian restaurants in the U.S.A. But don't make your reservations for Italy expecting to find it there because you won't. We're talking American Italian through and through.

If you're into gooey, cheesy, rich one-dish meals, then get going! Add Caesar salad (page 72) and garlic toast and you're ready to feed anyone.

This, like a good spaghetti sauce, is even better the next day. Stick it under the broiler and throw it on toast, and you've got instant breakfast, lunch, or dinner depending on your mood.

1 large eggplant, peeled and sliced into ½-inch slices
2 tsp salt
3 egg whites
½ cup nonfat yogurt
2 cups seasoned bread crumbs
1 onion, chopped
½ lb mushrooms, sliced
1 tsp garlic powder
½ tsp pepper
1 tsp Italian seasoning
1 tsp onion powder
½ tsp salt
3 cups tomato sauce or jarred marinara sauce
  Olive oil spray
2 cups shredded nonfat mozzarella cheese
1 cup nonfat Parmesan cheese

Preheat oven to 375 degrees.

Place eggplant in a colander. Sprinkle with salt and set aside for 20 minutes. Rinse and pat dry. Combine egg whites and yogurt. Dip eggplant slices in mixture and then into bread crumbs. Sauté onion and mushrooms on medium-high heat in a pan for 8–10 minutes or until onions are translucent and mushrooms release their juices. Add seasonings and tomato sauce, and simmer for 5 minutes. Spray nonstick skillet with olive oil spray and cook eggplant slices until crisped. This will take several batches. Spray pan in between each batch. Place eggplant in shallow baking dish, layer with cheeses and sauce, and top with cheese. Bake at 375 degrees for 1 hour or until sauce is bubbling and crust begins to form.

Nutritional:

Serving Size 14 ounces
Servings per Recipe 6
Calories 406
Total Fat 6.65 grams
Saturated Fat 1.10 grams

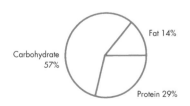

Fat 14%
Carbohydrate 57%
Protein 29%

Eggplant and Peppers

Side dish.

Topping for rice or pasta.

Put it in or on your Western Omelet (see page 144).

Make a sandwich out of it.

Whatever you can think of doing with eggplant, peppers, onions, garlic, broth, and seasonings all cooked together—DO IT, because this tastes great on or over anything.

The Italians eat sausage and peppers. Take out the tomatoes, add some eggplant—I've Americanized this great dish for my all-American cookbook.

Fab Idea

Brown Italian turkey sausage. Add the eggplant and other ingredients after the sausage is browned. Yuuummm.

1 medium eggplant, peeled, cut into ½-inch slices crosswise, and into strips ½-inch in diameter
½ red bell pepper, seeded and cut into ¼-inch-wide strips
½ green bell pepper, cut into ¼-inch-wide strips
1 medium onion, cut in half and thinly sliced
1 large clove garlic, minced
1 cup vegetable broth
1 tbsp rice vinegar
1 tsp Nature's Seasonings
1 tsp Mrs. Dash
1 tbsp chopped fresh parsley

Place cut eggplant in a colander in the sink or over a bowl. Salt generously and let stand about 10 minutes. Rinse thoroughly.

In a nonstick skillet over high heat, cook eggplant until browned. Add remaining vegetables, and cook until crisp-tender. Add broth, vinegar, and seasonings.

Sprinkle with parsley and serve over rice or pasta.

Nutritional:

Serving Size 5 ounces
Servings per Recipe 6
Calories 34.8
Total Fat 0.363 gram
Saturated Fat 0.035 gram

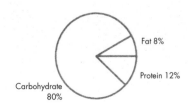

Fat 8%
Protein 12%
Carbohydrate 80%

Green Bean Casserole

Hey, Midwest: I've got your basic casserole with crispy fried things on the top, defatted and tasting a bit better than the old high-fat version. All you gotta do is say Green Bean Casserole and you know that it's the perfect

One-dish meal with tossed salad . . .
Side dish for chicken . . .
Potluck like you've never . . .

Nineties Green Bean Casserole update: TRAVELING FOOD.
To the park.
Weekend camp-out.
Any potluck.
Fab alternative to high-fat fast-food joints when you're starving and running everyone everywhere. Pack it up and go.

2 tbsp cornstarch
1 cup nonfat milk
½ cup mushroom liquid
1 cup nonfat sour cream
1 Knorr vegetable bouillon cube, dissolved in 2 tbsp water
1 tsp garlic powder
1 tsp Nature's Seasonings or salt
½ cup dried chopped onions
1 1-lb bag frozen French-cut green beans, thawed
2 4-oz cans mushrooms (net drained), liquid reserved
¾ cup bread crumbs
Butter-flavored spray

Preheat oven to 375 degrees.

Dissolve cornstarch in milk and stir over medium heat until thickened. Add mushroom liquid, sour cream, bouillon, and spices. Stir for 1 minute. Turn off heat and add half of onions.

Microwave or cook beans according to package directions. Drain, put beans in a casserole dish, and add mushrooms. Add sauce and top with bread crumbs and remaining onions. Spray with butter flavoring. Bake for 40 minutes, until golden and bubbling.

Nutritional:

Serving Size 11 ounces
Servings per Recipe 6
Calories 136
Total Fat 0.777 gram
Saturated Fat 0.185 gram

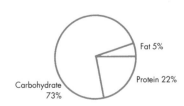

Fat 5%

Protein 22%

Carbohydrate 73%

Green Onion Dumplings

Dumplings—very American?

Like matzoh balls are American!!!

It may be a stretch, but these light—the lightest ever made —fabulous-tasting dumplings are perfect with your favorite low-fat broth, served with Chicken Fricassee (see page 96), or just eaten as is.

4 cups vegetable or chicken broth
5 tbsp flour, lightly browned in nonstick pot that has been
   sprayed with oil
1 cup all-purpose flour
2 tsp baking powder
1 egg
1 egg white
⅓ cup nonfat milk
1–2 tsp minced green onions

In large soup pot, combine broth and browned flour, and stir with a whisk until slightly thickened. (It may be necessary to add water during cooking process.) Mix in flour and baking powder. Mix in egg, egg whites, and milk. Add onions and combine thoroughly. Batter should be stiff.

Bring broth to a soft boil over medium-high heat. Drop batter by tablespoonsful into broth. Do not crowd the pot because the dumplings increase in volume as they cook. Cover and simmer for 5 minutes. Turn the dumplings over, cover, and simmer another 5 minutes. Serve immediately.

Nutritional:

Serving Size 8 ounces
Servings per Recipe 6
Calories 134
Total Fat 1.79 grams
Saturated Fat 0.317 gram

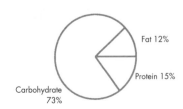

Fat 12%

Protein 15%

Carbohydrate
73%

Stuffed Peppers

Green and red peppers stuffed with black beans, rice, corn, green onions, and the perfect combination of spices—this dish couldn't be prettier and would be hard to beat in the taste department.

A one-dish meal.

Perfect side dish with anything.

Easy to turn into a meat dish just by adding ½ pound of ground lean turkey browned with chopped onions and mixed in with your pepper stuffing.

8 large red or green bell peppers (red are sweeter), tops and seeds removed
4 cups water
2 bouillon cubes
Olive oil spray
½ cup chopped green onion
2 cloves garlic, minced
3 cups uncooked rice
3 cups V-8 juice
3 cups vegetable broth
1 tsp Nature's Seasonings
1 15-oz can black beans, drained and rinsed
2 cups frozen corn
¼ cup chopped cilantro
¼ cup chopped parsley

In a pot large enough to hold the peppers, boil water and bouillon cube. Add peppers, lower heat, and simmer for 5 minutes. Drain, reserving liquid.

In a medium size pot sprayed with olive oil, sauté onion, garlic, and rice for 3 minutes. (It is important to cook rice in a pot. Be sure not to use a shallow pan as rice may scorch during cooking time.) Add the V-8 juice, broth, and Nature's Seasonings. Bring to a boil, then lower to simmer. Cover and cook 15–20 minutes or until rice is tender. Remove from heat. Stir in the beans, corn, and herbs.

Stuff peppers with mixture. Put a tablespoon of the cooking liquid from peppers over each stuffed pepper. Put in baking dish. Surround the peppers with any remaining stuffing and drizzle cooking liquid over the stuffing until bottom of dish is a little soupy. Bake covered at 375 degrees for 20 minutes or until peppers can be easily pierced with a fork.

Serve with Creamy Lemon Herb Sauce (see page 261).

Nutritional:

Serving Size 19 ounces
Servings per Recipe 8
Calories 379
Total Fat 1.44 grams
Saturated Fat 0.234 gram

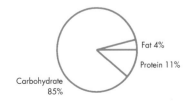

Fat 4%
Protein 11%
Carbohydrate 85%

Down-home
Mashed Potatoes

I have a bit of a potato issue that I'd like to bring up before we get into the best mashed potato dish you've ever had.

Why have Idaho and its potato-producing power been left out of the internationally recognized history of potatoes?

Maybe the Irish went through a revolution or two and only had potatoes to eat, and we started with the big turkey festival.

I'd like to say that I still think IDAHO DESERVES A PLACE RIGHT NEXT TO THE WORLD POTATO PRODUCERS.

Having said that, and feeling much better for it, let's get on with the recipe. The perfect side dish, anyone???

Anytime.

Anywhere.

Always satisfying.

What's more comforting than mashed potatoes?

Make 'em and taste 'em. They speak for themselves. This is proof that you can have your favorite taste and texture and cut the fat without an ounce of effort.

If you've got friends who whine and moan that you have to eat rabbit food in order to get leaner and healthier, shove these potatoes in their mouths.

Leftovers

Potato pancakes for breakfast, anyone? Nobody on earth would turn that down. Shape your refrigerated leftover potatoes into patties, dip 'em into bread crumbs, and fry 'em up in the old nonstick, very American frying pan (one of our favorite utensils in the new and improved thigh-slimming kitchen).

And remember: Potatoes in a big pot of anything thicken and flavor it in a heartbeat and are a great meal stretcher.

6 medium-large potatoes, cut into 1-inch cubes
2 garlic cloves, coarsely chopped
1 medium onion, finely chopped
³/₄ cup nonfat sour cream
¹/₂ cup nonfat milk
1 tbsp Butter Buds
1 tbsp Nature's Seasonings
¹/₈ tsp white pepper

Additional options:
¹/₄ cup chopped parsley
¹/₄ cup chopped green onions
    Sweated onions (onions cooked over medium-high heat in a
    nonstick pan until limp and golden brown)

Place potatoes (with the skin left on for flavor and added nutritional benefits), garlic, and onion in a pot and cover with water. Boil until a fork breaks a potato easily. Drain and return to the pot. Add the sour cream, milk, butter, and seasonings. Mash together until creamy, leaving in a few lumps for texture.

Nutritional:

Serving Size 6 ounces
Servings per Recipe 6
Calories 172
Total Fat 0.28 gram
Saturated Fat 0.088 gram

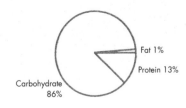

Fat 1%

Protein 13%

Carbohydrate
86%

Cheesy Sour Cream Potatoes

How good does this sound? Think about it: You've got the barbecue on. The chef's apron wrapped around you. The flag raised (on the flagpole in your backyard). The burgers are done. And when it's time, you fill the plate with Cheesy Sour Cream Potatoes and whatever else you want to serve (nothing is going to be able to upstage this dish, so don't put too much energy into things like coleslaw). It's a hit.

Morning

Guess what else you can do with this little cheesy potato-ey number? Breakfast.

Oh, sure. . . .

Scramble up some egg whites and load 'em onto a pile of these potatoes.

Cobb Salad

Oven-fried Chicken

Chicken Fricassee

Nonfat Vegetarian Lasagna

Chewy **E**asy **P**izza

Prune **A**pricot **B**utter

Chili **B**eans, **B**order **S**tyle

Polenta with **M**ushroom **S**auce

Chocolate **B**read **P**udding

Cherry **P**each **C**obbler

Cheesy Sour Cream Potatoes

Stawberry, Blueberry, Pear Mold

Grilled **V**egetable **M**edley

Lemon **C**heesecake

Shrimp Creole

Meatloaf

4 medium russet potatoes, cut into 6 wedges each
  Nonstick cooking spray
1 tbsp Mrs. Dash onion herb seasoning
1/2 tsp salt
1/2 tsp pepper
2 cups grated nonfat cheddar cheese
1/2 cup nonfat sour cream
2 tbsp chopped green onions
1 tbsp chopped parsley

Boil potatoes until just tender. Do not overcook or they will fall apart. Preheat oven to 400 degrees. Spray shallow baking dish with nonstick spray. Place potatoes in baking dish, sprinkle with herb mixture, salt, and pepper. Place in oven about 35–40 minutes, until brown. Sprinkle with cheese. Bake 5 minutes more, or until cheese is melted. Pour sour cream on top. Sprinkle with green onions and parsley.

Nutritional:

Serving Size 5 ounces
Servings per Recipe 6
Calories 167
Total Fat 0.107 gram
Saturated Fat 0.028 gram

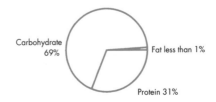

Carbohydrate 69%

Fat less than 1%

Protein 31%

Spicy Oven Fries

One of my favorites. Had a bunch while I was on the phone the other day and couldn't get enough.

These thin strips of potatoes, tossed in spices and baked on a cookie sheet, ARE French fries. No doubt about it, we're talking good fries. Crispy, salty, spicy. (Not interested in spice on your fries? Don't put it on, just salt 'em up.)

Good project for the kids and some great eatin' for everyone.

Nonstick spray
1 large potato, cut into ¼-inch strips
2 tsp Nature's Seasonings

Preheat oven to 500 degrees. Spray foil-covered cookie sheet with nonstick spray. Toss potatoes in seasonings. Put on cookie sheet and bake for 20 minutes, turning once, or until brown and crisp.

Nutritional:

Serving Size 6.8 ounces
Servings per Recipe 1
Calories 206
Total Fat 0.254 gram
Saturated Fat 0.071 gram

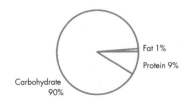

Fat 1%
Protein 9%
Carbohydrate 90%

Potato Skins

Start your own T.G.I. Betty's with this recipe.

Potato skins: Salty, cheesy, not dripping in oil. Tasty, tasty, tasty to top with:

Salsa
Black beans
Grilled veggies
Some of our nonfried, fried chicken

That's what I wanted when I said, "Get me a potato skin." A skin that would work as an appetizer or just as well as a fabulous side dish.

A skin that would make a great late-night snack, just as good for breakfast. (Sure, with scrambled egg whites in "nature's dish.")

You make a batch of these skins and tell me. Did we make a potato skin good enough to serve in our own T.G.I.'s and everywhere else? Every mom that tasted ours thought we did!!!

4 medium russet potatoes, scrubbed
¼ cup nonfat sour cream
½ cup nonfat shredded cheese, cheddar preferred
2 tbsp parsley, chopped
4 slices turkey bacon, cooked till crisp, and crumbled
2 tsp onion powder
2 tsp Nature's Seasonings

Preheat oven to 500 degrees.

Microwave potatoes about 4 minutes, until soft, or bake potatoes at 400 degrees for 40 minutes, until potatoes can be broken easily with a fork. Split in half lengthwise and scoop out pulp, leaving ¼-inch shell.

Divide sour cream among shells, sprinkle cheese over each, parsley, bacon, onion powder, and Nature's Seasonings.

Bake in 500-degree oven 10–15 minutes, uncovered, until browned.

Nutritional:

Serving Size 4 ounces
Servings per Recipe 4
Calories 197
Total Fat 2.09 grams
Saturated Fat 0.691 gram

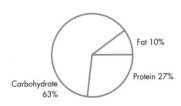

Fat 10%

Protein 27%

Carbohydrate 63%

Potato Wedges

Ever heard of steak fries?

Did you ever dream of having steak fries without the dripping grease? You've got it.

Anything you'd do with steak fries, do with these.

They are fabulous . . .
    With baked chicken
    With fish sticks
    Plain, with Mushroom Onion Gravy (see page 274)
    As a leftover in the morning with egg whites and toast.

Word of Advice

Double this recipe. You won't believe how good these taste thawed. Freeze them in a plastic bag, pull them out, and stick them under the broiler for a few minutes.

Dip these in ketchup, Green Goddess Dressing (see page 76), or anything else you want to dip them into. Take my word for it: You're going to be a potato wedge-eating American citizen. And I'm not—yet. But I want to be . . . please.

½ cup bread crumbs
1 tbsp Cajun seasoning or Spike seasoning or Nature's
   Seasonings
1 tsp garlic powder
1 tsp onion powder
6 medium potatoes, cut lengthwise into 6 wedges each
2 egg whites, beaten

Preheat oven to 450 degrees.

Combine bread crumbs and spices in a bag. Dip potato wedges in egg whites, coating thoroughly. Toss in crumb mixture and coat completely. Place on a baking sheet lightly sprayed with nonstick spray. Bake about 35 minutes, until crisp and brown.

Nutritional:

Serving Size 4 ounces
Servings per Recipe 6
Calories 153
Total Fat 0.328 gram
Saturated Fat 0.084 gram

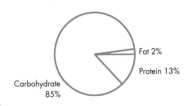

Fat 2%

Protein 13%

Carbohydrate 85%

Twice Baked Potatoes

In the mood for creamy, cheesy, buttery? Want something that is great anytime? Something that works for breakfast, lunch, dinner, snack? We're talking potatoes stuffed with broccoli, nonfat sour cream, nonfat cheddar cheese, and spices. I'm in. I'm there when these potatoes are being served. Great for anything, anytime.

4 medium russet potatoes, scrubbed
¼ cup vegetable broth
½ cup nonfat sour cream
1 cup frozen or fresh broccoli, cooked until just tender but still
   bright green
1 tsp Butter Buds
½ tsp salt
½ tsp white pepper
1 cup shredded nonfat cheddar cheese

Bake potatoes in 400-degree oven for 35 minutes, or until done. Or microwave 15–20 minutes. Cool, cut in half lengthwise, and scoop out pulp, leaving ¼ inch of potato inside skin. Put pulp in bowl with broth and sour cream. Mash. Add broccoli, butter, salt, pepper, and cheese. Fill potato skins. Return to 400-degree oven for 15 minutes, or until top is brown. Serve with Bacon Gravy (see page 272) or nonfat sour cream.

Nutritional:

Serving Size 7½ ounces
Servings per Recipe 4
Calories 209
Total Fat 0.272 gram
Saturated Fat 0.05 gram

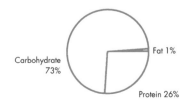

Fat 1%

Carbohydrate
73%

Protein 26%

Grilled Vegetable Medley

Ahhhhh, grilled.

Barbecues.

The smell of it, the feel of it, the taste of it.

It's so us, don't you think? Does anyone else in the world grill?

In the past when you thought of grilled, you thought burger, dog (not as in family pet, as in hot), and if you ever even considered grilled veggies, it was as the stepsister of everything else being grilled.

Well, not anymore.

These grilled veggies taste great and take up the whole barbecue, so put them in the forefront (it's about time) and make the saturated fat and cholesterol take a backseat to what should always have been the star of the grill event . . .

 ssssst . . .

Here's a grill food you can marinate in a bag and take with you to the friends' or relatives' or birthday grill-out.

These grillers taste great with anything you're having for dinner. . . . Stick 'em under the broiler on a baking pan and do your grilling in-house.

Make a grilled veggie sandwich. I just made one the other day. It was fabulous.

Thick bread
Mustard
Grilled veggies
Sauerkraut

The best!!!!

Marinade
- ½ cup lemon juice
- 2 tbsp olive oil
- 4 cloves garlic, crushed
- 2 tsp Italian seasoning
- 1½ tsp Spike seasoning

- 6 red potatoes, boiled until tender
- 2 medium zucchini, sliced ¼-inch thick lengthwise
- 2 red or green bell peppers, seeded and sliced lengthwise into ½-inch or 1-inch strips
- 2 red onions, sliced across the grain into ⅓-inch-thick pieces
- ½ lb mushrooms
- 1 large eggplant, peeled and sliced into ½-inch-thick pieces

Combine lemon juice, olive oil, and seasonings. Pour over vegetables in a big bowl. Let marinate for at least one hour, longer if possible.

Cook over hot coals approximately 10 minutes on each side.

Serve over hot brown rice and pour remaining marinade over all.

Nutritional:

Serving Size 11 ounces
Servings per Recipe 6
Calories 148
Total Fat 5.07 grams
Saturated Fat 0.699 gram

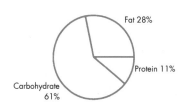

Fat 28%
Protein 11%
Carbohydrate 61%

187

Sautéed Vegetable Sticks

Had to do something to improve the reputation of the sautéed veggie! This recipe does the trick. Take something good that always tasted kind of bland and make it easy and perfect-tasting every time. Call it Sautéed Vegetable Sticks.

¾ cup vegetable broth
2 parsnips, peeled and cut into sticks ¼-inch wide and 2 inches long
2 carrots, cut same as above
1 zucchini, cut same as above
1 yellow squash, cut same as above
2 tbsp minced green onion
2 tbsp minced parsley
2 tbsp lemon juice
½ tsp Nature's Seasonings

Place broth, parsnips, and carrots in a shallow pan and cook, covered, over medium high heat for about 5 minutes. Add zucchini and squash, and cook 2 minutes more. Add water if necessary. Toss with remaining ingredients. Serve over rice.

Nutritional:

Serving Size 6.3 ounces
Servings per Recipe 4
Calories 57.3
Total Fat 0.464 gram
Saturated Fat 0.061 gram

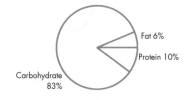

Fat 6%
Protein 10%
Carbohydrate 83%

Zucchini Corn Cakes

Suspicious? Understandably so. "Zucchini" and "cake" together? Scary. But don't worry, because these are great.

$\mathcal{I}$deas from the Chef

Serve these at breakfast with Bacon Gravy (see page 272). Or cook crumbled turkey bacon in the batter.

Or pour on some Basic Cream Sauce (page 258) with a squeeze of lemon.

Yeah, you're getting it. All-American Zucchini Corn Cakes coming right up!

2 cups grated zucchini
1 cup frozen corn
¼ cup finely chopped red bell pepper
   Salt
½ cup flour
3 egg whites, beaten
½ tsp baking powder
¼ cup nonfat milk
2 tbsp rice vinegar
1 tsp Spike Seasoning
⅛ tsp white pepper
   Oil for spray
2 tbsp chopped green onion
2 tbsp chopped parsley

Combine zucchini, corn, and bell pepper in a colander or strainer over a bowl. Sprinkle with salt and let sit 30 minutes. Rinse with cold water and squeeze dry.

Combine flour, egg whites, baking powder, milk, vinegar, ½ teaspoon of salt, and other seasonings. Add vegetables.

Drop by spoonfuls onto a hot nonstick skillet that has been lightly sprayed with oil. Brown on both sides.

Serve sprinkled with onion and parsley.

Nutritional:

Serving Size 4.3 ounces
Servings per Recipe 6
Calories 82.2
Total Fat 0.235 gram
Saturated Fat 0.051 gram

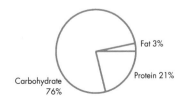

Fat 3%

Protein 21%

Carbohydrate 76%

*Reading this title should get you healthier . . .
what more could you want if healthy bowels are
something you're interested in??? Healthy
bowels are fine, and very necessary, but it's taste,
ease in preparation, and getting the kids to eat
that we are much more concerned with, and
taking a category of food like rice, beans,
breads, and grains and making it make sense
wasn't easy, but there's nothing our taste-testing
moms can't handle and handle they did. Throw
in a rice or bean recipe once in a while, and
adjust your eating a bit to include these
wonderful foods.*

Rice and Beans, Breads and Grains

Basic Vegetarian Rice

One of the most important meals in the book.
Make a ton and keep it in the fridge to use all week.

Because you can
  throw it in soup.
  put it underneath anything.
  warm it up and eat it alone with some soy sauce (very, very American—a bowl of rice and soy sauce?). Rice in the fridge has saved me every time I run in the door and see hungry children waiting to be fed.
  Rice and . . . EVERYTHING.

2 cups uncooked long grain rice
4 cups vegetable broth
1 tsp Spike seasoning
½ tsp Nature's Seasoning

Cook rice in vegetable broth per package directions, adding spices to the liquid.

For herb rice add 1 tablespoon chopped parsley, 1 tablespoon chopped green onion, 1 tablespoon fines herbes or 1 tablespoon fresh basil.

Nutritional:

Serving Size 7.8 ounces
Servings per Recipe 6
Calories 246
Total Fat 0.421 gram
Saturated Fat 0.115 gram

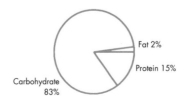

Fat 2%
Protein 15%
Carbohydrate 83%

Confetti Rice

I ordered this dish in a restaurant the other night, and it didn't touch our version. I don't ever want to be a cookbook writing snob, but the truth is the truth.

Rice mixed with lots and lots of zucchini, corn, red bell pepper, red onion, peas, herbs, and spices:

Colorful, fast, great alone or alongside anything.
One of the best omelet stuffers you can get.
Brilliant way to get the kids to eat their veggies.
Potluck city.

An all-around good dish!!

1 cup rice
1 1/3 cups water or broth
1 tsp salt
1 tsp garlic powder
1 cup cut carrots, very thin 2-inch-long strips
1/2 cup chopped red onion
1 cup cut zucchini, 1/4-inch squares
1/2 cup frozen corn kernels
1/2 cup diced red bell peppers
1/2 cup frozen peas
2 tbsp chopped parsley
1 tbsp thyme or marjoram

Place rice, water, salt, and garlic powder in a pot with a tight-fitting lid. Bring to a boil, then lower heat to simmer. After 10 minutes add carrots and onion. Steam another 5 minutes, then add remaining vegetables.

Remove from heat, leaving lid on another 5 minutes. Fluff rice and distribute vegetables throughout rice. Sprinkle with herbs and serve.

Nutritional:

Serving Size 3 ounces
Servings per Recipe 12
Calories 76.9
Total Fat 0.268 gram
Saturated Fat 0.054 gram

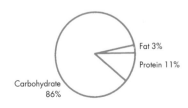

Fat 3%
Protein 11%
Carbohydrate 86%

San Francisco Rice

Rice-A-Roni but better. What dinner wouldn't want this as a side dish?

There's no grilling that's complete unless this Roni of a Rice specialty is sitting next to it.

Sitting down alone after a long, hard day with a huge bowl of San Francisco Rice in front of me and chowing down ... plain, simple, easy, and tasty.

        Nonstick spray
    1 cup sliced mushrooms
    1 clove garlic, chopped
    1 medium onion, chopped
    1 cup uncooked rice
    1 cup fine noodles
2½ cups vegetable or chicken broth
    1 tsp Mrs. Dash onion and herb mix
    1 tsp Mrs. Dash garlic and herb mix
    ½ tsp salt
    1 tbsp finely chopped parsley

In a skillet sprayed with nonstick spray, sauté the mushrooms, garlic, and onion. Remove from pan and set aside.
Add rice and noodles to the pan and cook until the rice
becomes translucent. Return mushroom mixture to the pan.
Add broth, bring to a boil, lower the heat, and add seasonings. Cover and cook until the rice is tender, about 20 minutes.

Nutritional:

Serving Size 6.6 ounces
Servings per Recipe 6
Calories 167
Total Fat 0.869 gram
Saturated Fat 0.092 gram

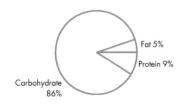

Fat 5%

Protein 9%

Carbohydrate
86%

Red and Black Beans with Rice

Oh, yeah. This is about as swampy as it gets when you're talking Cajun. Spicy, hot, exotic, and a jazzy, jazzy version of the old swamp favorite, Red and Black Beans with Rice.

I know what I'm talking about when it comes to swamps. My sons and I just got back from one—alligator hunting on the hottest swamp ever. Couldn't even think of being Americanized without going out on a swampy limb and testing my strength in the elements, looking at the alligator eye to eye, seeing what I was really made of.

In Florida,

On a private boat,

With two private instructors,

Looking at water lilies.

Not *too* cush.

So, wouldn't you say that qualifies me to talk about the New Orleans swamp specialty Red and Black Beans with Rice?

At least let me give you some great suggestions for this great, rib-sticking, spicy meal that serves a crowd. This will feed sixteen of the hungriest.

Leftovers

Leftovers Lover's Dream is what this dish is . . .

You can instantly convert this dish from Cajun to Mexican by reheating it and wrapping it in a tortilla.

Another thought: Stuff this in your omelet (or use that expression the next time you want to insult the hell out of someone) or just have your Red and Black Beans with Rice as a great side dish to anything. Who doesn't need a little spice on the side of the plate every once in a while?

½ lb each dried small black beans and red beans
1 cup each chopped green onions, chopped celery, and
 chopped onion
4 garlic cloves, chopped
½ lb smoked turkey sausage, cut lengthwise and then into
 ⅛-inch slices
¾ cup diced turkey ham (¼-inch dice)
6–8 cups defatted chicken or vegetable broth
1 tsp Nature's Seasonings (Morton's brand)
1 tsp dried red pepper

Soak beans overnight in water. Drain and return to pot.

Sweat vegetables in a nonstick pan until translucent, about 2–3 minutes. Add to beans in pot.

Cook sausage and ham in same pan, adding ½ cup of broth after the meat is browned to release the little brown bits, about 5 minutes.

Add meat and seasonings to pot, cover with broth, and bring to a boil. Lower to simmer and cook, covered, for 1½ hours or until beans are tender and sauce is creamy.

Serve with rice cooked in vegetable broth.

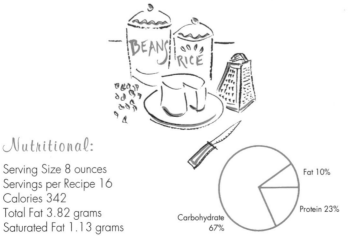

Nutritional:

Serving Size 8 ounces
Servings per Recipe 16
Calories 342
Total Fat 3.82 grams
Saturated Fat 1.13 grams

Fat 10%
Protein 23%
Carbohydrate 67%

Mexican Rice Casserole

Here's to the Alamo. Santa Anna would have kept fighting for this, and as Travis would say, drawing the line in the sand, everyone who wants to eat this dish, cross this line.

Get ready, because you can expect a full-course meal here.

Everywhere you look tacos, chilies, and burritos are topping the charts of America's favorite foods. Spanish is our second language now. I just left Miami airport, and nobody understood what I was saying in English!

Serve this *cacerola de l'arroz* with some iced tea and a side of salsa, and you're in. Hip and spicy, with a very meal-in-a-bowl nineties kind of feel.

Leftovers

Just as is, this dish is a leftover dream.

Heat it up, toss a salad, and you've got instant dinner for four to six people. Grab yourself some low-fat tortilla chips and dip and eat, dip and eat, dip and eat . . .

1½ cups uncooked rice
  Nonstick spray
1 tsp olive oil
1 cup chopped onion
1 garlic clove, minced
½ cup chopped celery
½ cup chopped green pepper
¾ lb lean ground beef
1 4-oz can Old El Paso green chilies (mild), drained and
  chopped
1 tsp basil
¾ tsp salt
½ tsp black pepper
1 15-oz can red beans, rinsed and drained
1 15-oz can Hunt's tomato sauce, diluted with ½ cup broth

Preheat oven to 350 degrees.

Cook rice according to package directions. Spray baking dish (8 inches by 8 inches) and set aside.

Heat oil in a nonstick pot and sauté onions until soft. Add garlic, celery, and green pepper, and cook a few minutes longer. Add ground beef and green chilies, and cook until meat changes color. Add basil, salt, pepper, beans, and half of the tomato sauce mixture. Cook until blended together.

Spread half of the rice in a baking dish. Cover with meat mixture. Cover meat mixture with balance of rice and pour remaining tomato mixture over all. Bake in 350-degree oven for 30 to 45 minutes.

Nutritional:

Serving Size 12 ounces
Servings per Recipe 8
Calories 380
Total Fat 7.47 grams
Saturated Fat 2.62 grams

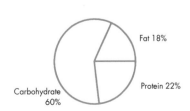

Fat 18%

Protein 22%

Carbohydrate
60%

Corn, Lima, and Black Bean Pudding

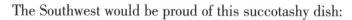

The Southwest would be proud of this succotashy dish:

It's a casserole.
It's a one-dish meal.
It's the take-along dish of all time.

Put it all together, baked with a golden bread crumb crust, and enjoy.

1 10-oz package (2 cups) frozen baby lima beans
1 cup petite frozen corn
½ cup rinsed and drained black beans
2 tsp Nature's Seasonings, or ½ tsp salt and ½ tsp pepper
2 cups nonfat evaporated milk
1 egg, beaten
2 egg whites, beaten
2 tbsp finely chopped green onion
2 tbsp finely chopped parsley
   Nonstick spray
1 cup fresh bread crumbs
   Oil

Preheat oven to 375 degrees.

Place lima beans, corn, and black beans in a pot with Nature's Seasonings and 1 cup of milk. Bring to a boil. Turn heat to low and cook for 5 minutes. Remove from heat.

Beat egg, egg whites, and remaining ingredients together (except bread crumbs) and combine with bean-corn mixture.

Pour into an 9-by-9-inch dish sprayed with nonstick spray. Put bread crumbs on top and spray lightly with oil.

Bake at 375 degrees for 20–30 minutes, or until bread crumbs are browned and pudding is set.

Serve with nonfat sour cream or Fresh Tomato Sauce (see page 254) on the side.

Nutritional:

Serving Size 7½
Servings per Recipe 6
Calories 194
Total Fat 1.5 grams
Saturated Fat 0.457 gram

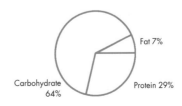

Fat 7%

Carbohydrate 64%

Protein 29%

Boston Baked Beans

If you've ever wanted to go back to the old settler tradition of baking beans on Saturday and serving 'em up on Sunday for breakfast with codfish cakes and Boston brown bread, then this is the place to start.

We're talking navy beans baked for hours with molasses and turkey bacon.

We're talking Boston Baked Beans—
    the perfect meal on toast
    the best barbecue side dish
    a great "quick salad, bread, and beans" kind of dish.

2 cups dried navy or white beans
6 slices turkey bacon, diced
2 medium onions, finely chopped
1/3 cup light brown sugar
3 tbsp unsulfured molasses
1 tsp salt
1/2 tsp dried mustard
1/8 tsp pepper
1/4 cup chili sauce

Cook beans according to package directions until tender. Reserve 2 cups of their cooking liquid.

Cook bacon and onions for about 5 minutes until onions are soft. Add to beans, combining well.

Add remaining ingredients and stir well. Pour reserved bean liquid over beans, combining thoroughly.

Bake at 300 degrees in covered casserole for 2 hours. Remove cover and bake until sauce on top begins to form crust, about 1/2 hour.

Nutritional:

Serving Size 6 ounces
Servings per Recipe 8
Calories 223
Total Fat 2.14 grams
Saturated Fat 0.65 gram

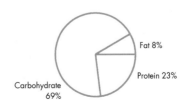

Fat 8%

Protein 23%

Carbohydrate
69%

Chili Beans, Border Style

What border do you think they were talking about when they (the recipe experts of the world) invented this dish? Our borders: The U.S. of A. at its best.

And this isn't just any old border dish. Four stars on this one.

Our taste-testing moms loved it. They were scooping out the beans with spoons, chips, fingers, whatever was available just to get to the great beany taste of this new border dish.

Serving Suggestions

Soup or dip (just add low-fat chips, and you've got that down)

With grilled veggies
With chicken
With fish

This pot of southwestern flavors is great any way you down it.

1 medium onion, chopped
2 cloves garlic, mashed
¼ cup chopped green bell pepper
1 15-oz can black beans, drained and rinsed
1 15-oz can small white beans
2 4-oz cans chopped green chilis
1 28-oz can chopped or whole tomatoes
1 tsp cumin
½ tsp chili powder
Salt and pepper to taste
Chopped green onion, nonfat sour cream, and shredded
nonfat cheddar cheese for garnish

Sweat onions, garlic, and bell pepper in a large pot. Add remaining ingredients except garnish and simmer for at least 30 minutes.

Garnish with chopped green onion, nonfat sour cream, and shredded nonfat cheddar cheese.

Nutritional:

Serving Size 10½ ounces
Servings per Recipe 6
Calories 143
Total Fat 1.18 grams
Saturated Fat 0.146 gram

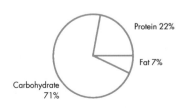

Protein 22%

Fat 7%

Carbohydrate 71%

Cornbread

Cornbread and the settlers.
Cornbread and chili.
Cornbread and

Picnics
Barbecues
The Deep South
Ordering iced coffee and corn muffins for breakfast . . .
Oh, EXCUSE ME, a bit of personal history:

Every morning when I was working in New York, I'd order iced coffee and a corn muffin (the North's version of cornbread) first thing in the morning.
Loved it then. Still do now. When it's

Hot
Corny
With honey dripping down the sides

Cornbread and anything. . . .

Fab Ideas

Try adding shredded cheese, chopped chilis, and cilantro; or chopped green onions and crumbled cooked turkey bacon; or chopped parsley.

1 cup all-purpose flour
1½ cups cornmeal
1 tsp brown sugar
½ tsp salt
¾ tsp baking soda
1 tbsp baking powder
1 cup buttermilk
1 cup creamed corn
3 egg whites, beaten
2 tbsp honey
1 tbsp Butter Buds

Preheat oven to 400 degrees.

Combine dry ingredients. Combine wet ingredients. Mix wet and dry ingredients together. Bake in nonstick 8-inch baking pan for approximately 30 minutes, or until it springs back when lightly touched in the center.

For Chili Cornbread Pie, eliminate the honey and add ½ tsp Mrs. Dash onion and herb seasoning.

Nutritional:

Serving Size 4 ounces
Servings per Recipe 8
Calories 196
Total Fat 0.988 gram
Saturated Fat 0.27 gram

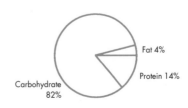

Fat 4%

Protein 14%

Carbohydrate 82%

Garlic Herb Bread

You go into an Italian restaurant having committed to your new low-fat life and bammo, you get slammed with the garlic bread the minute you walk in the door. Who can resist the stuff?

Now here's a solution for you. Make a batch of this, carry it in your purse, dump their garlic bread under the table, and put your new, fabulous-tasting, low-fat version in the little basket with the red napkin. They'll never know until you leave. Of course you probably can never go back to your favorite little Italian joint . . . I haven't figured out the solution to that yet, let you know when I do.

½ cup nonfat cottage cheese
2 cloves garlic, minced
3 tbsp parmesan cheese
1 tsp Nature's Seasonings
¼ cup nonfat milk
8 basil leaves, chopped fine, or 1 tbsp dried basil
2 tbsp Italian parsley, chopped fine, or 1 tbsp dried parsley
1 medium size loaf of French or sourdough bread

Combine all ingredients except bread, parsley, and basil in blender and pulse until blended, adding only enough milk to mix. Add parsley and basil to mixture.

Spread on slices of French or sourdough bread. Heat in 500-degree oven until browned, about 10 to 15 minutes.

Nutritional:

Serving Size 1.6 ounce
Servings per Recipe 12
Calories 93.7
Total Fat 1.34 grams
Saturated Fat 0.488 gram

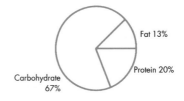

Fat 13%

Protein 20%

Carbohydrate 67%

Breakfast Burrito

My kind of breakfast.

There isn't anyone who wouldn't love this breakfast burrito, unless of course they have no taste (that's taste buds, not class). This, my friends—and hopefully countrymen—is a great, hearty all-in-one meal. Throw on some Salsa (see page 252) and you've got a premenstrual dream going on. I eat this anytime of the day or night because if it's got salt and spices in it, I'm there.

12 egg whites, beaten until frothy
   Oil
½ cup nonfat sour cream
1 cup nonfat cheddar cheese
½ cup refried beans
4 nonfat flour tortillas, burrito size
2 tbsp chopped cilantro
1 cup salsa
2 tbsp chopped green onion

Scramble egg whites in a nonstick pan lightly coated with oil. Combine eggs with sour cream and cheese.

Spread beans on each tortilla. Sprinkle with cilantro. Spoon egg mixture on top, in the center of tortilla. Fold in sides and roll up each tortilla.

Microwave for 30 seconds. Put salsa on top and sprinkle with remaining cilantro and onions. Serve with extra salsa and nonfat sour cream on the side.

Nutritional:

Serving Size 10½ ounces/1 burrito
Servings per Recipe 4
Calories 300
Total Fat 1.08 grams
Saturated Fat 0.164 gram

Fat 3%

Carbohydrate 63%

Protein 34%

French Toast Fingers

As if French Toast isn't good enough! The best breakfast in the land has just been made better.

$\mathcal{W}$ord to the Wise

Double this old favorite. You'll be eating leftovers, and it freezes great.

If you don't know how to serve French Toast, you should be a little concerned.

Serve it with hot maple syrup, fresh fruit sauce, or just a sprinkle of cinnamon. Try Blackberry Puree (see page 344) or Prune Apricot Butter (see page 278) over the top.

Yuuuummmm.

$\mathcal{P}$ssssst . . .

It's important in this recipe to use really thick bread, the thicker the better.

³/₄ cup nonfat milk
1 tsp vanilla extract
5 egg whites, beaten
¹/₂ tsp ground cinnamon
¹/₄ tsp nutmeg
2 tsp sugar or 1 tsp honey
¹/₄ tsp salt
6 slices day-old, slightly stale nonfat or low-fat bread, cut into
  2-inch-wide slices
  Oil for spray

Mix together wet ingredients and spices. Pour over bread in a shallow pan. Let soak 5–10 minutes. Heat a nonstick pan coated with a light spray of oil. Add bread pieces and brown both sides.

Nutritional:

Serving Size 4.5 ounces
Servings per Recipe 4
Calories 163
Total Fat 1.48 grams
Saturated Fat 0.396 gram

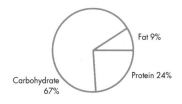

Fat 9%

Protein 24%

Carbohydrate
67%

Buttermilk Pancakes with Blueberries

Let me ask you: If you serve these up with hot maple syrup, hot blueberry sauce (got the recipe for ya right here), or the Orange Custard Sauce on page 332 . . . who's gonna complain?

Triple this batch and freeze it for a fast, fast breakfast or late-night snack. Replace the blueberries with diced apples, peaches, or bananas and you'll never want to go out for pancakes again, unless of course you just want to spend some cash and put on a few pounds.

1 cup unbleached or all-purpose flour
1 tbsp plus 1 tsp sugar
1 tsp baking powder
$^1/_2$ tsp baking soda
1 cup nonfat or low-fat buttermilk
2 tbsp nonfat mayonnaise
3 egg whites, beaten
$^1/_4$ cup nonfat milk
1 cup frozen blueberries
    Nonstick spray

Combine all dry ingredients, then combine all wet ingredients and mix together, adding blueberries last. Drop by spoonfuls onto hot skillet sprayed with nonstick spray or canola oil. Brown on both sides.

Blueberry Sauce

1 cup frozen blueberries, defrosted
$^1/_4$ cup sugar
$^1/_2$ tsp cinnamon

Combine in saucepan and heat through.

Nutritional:

Serving Size 2.7 ounces
Servings per Recipe 12
Calories 89.4
Total Fat 0.387 gram
Saturated Fat 0.141 gram

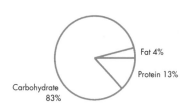

Fat 4%
Protein 13%
Carbohydrate 83%

Cheesy Bacon Grits

Yeah, yeah, yeah, I know. It's a miracle. Cheesy Bacon Grits done low fat.

Thank you. I'd like to thank the Academy . . . and my first cooking instructor, way back . . .

This delicious breakfast casserole is gonna win an award. I'm telling you, get the acceptance speech ready.

If you go to a truck stop (one of your usual daily stops) and order up some Cheesy Bacon Grits, you're talking 30 grams of fat per serving, but in your own kitchen truck stop, check it out.

Couldn't be better for a casual brunch, lunch, dinner, breakfast, snack, school, anything.

Try pouring on some Mushroom Onion Gravy (see page 274). Ten four, big guy.

4¼ cups nonfat milk
  1 cup quick-cooking grits
1½ tsp Molly McButter or Butter Buds
  1 tsp Nature's Seasonings
  5 egg whites, slightly beaten
  2 cups nonfat shredded cheddar cheese
  6 slices turkey bacon, cooked and crumbled
  4 drops hot pepper sauce
    Nonstick spray

Bring milk to a boil, add grits, reduce heat to simmer. Cook
5 minutes. Remove from heat. Add Molly McButter, Nature's
Seasonings, and egg whites. Stir in 1½ cups cheese, bacon,
and hot pepper sauce. Turn into 8-by-8-inch baking pan
sprayed with nonstick spray. Sprinkle with remaining cheese
and bake in 375-degree oven for 45 minutes, till brown and
puffy.

Option: add ⅛ cup chopped green onion, or ⅛ cup
chopped parsley.

Nutritional:

Serving Size 10 ounces
Servings per Recipe 6
Calories 281
Total Fat 2.62 grams
Saturated Fat 0.914 gram

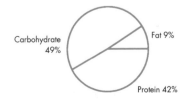

Carbohydrate 49%
Fat 9%
Protein 42%

Raisin Multigrain Oat Cakes

Could this recipe have any more ingredients that are good for us in the title? Forget about everything you've ever thought about oats and think about one thing: the best stick-to-your-ribs pancakes, served with maple syrup or your very favorite Prune Apricot Butter (see page 278). Then think about how much you are going to enjoy lying in bed on a lazy Sunday morning and eating 'em. (Even if the last time you did something like that was years ago, there's nothing wrong with thinking about it!!!)

$\mathcal{P}$sssst . . .

Triple the batch and store in plastic bags in the freezer. The minute you're in the mood for this taste treat, all you have to do is pop them out and put 'em in the toaster. A quick breakfast, a great snack—what could be easier?

¾ cup flour
1 cup multigrain cereal or oatmeal (Quaker quick-cooking)
1 tsp baking powder
¼ cup brown sugar
1 tsp ground cinnamon
¼ cup raisins
1 egg, beaten
2 egg whites, beaten
½–¾ cup milk
Nonstick spray

Combine dry ingredients. Combine wet ingredients. Mix wet and dry together. Let sit at least 15 minutes or overnight. Spray a shallow frying pan with nonstick spray. Ladle batter onto pan in 4-inch rounds. Cook over medium-high heat about 2 minutes per side, or until golden brown.

Nutritional:

Serving Size 4.3 ounces
Servings per Recipe 4
Calories 263
Total Fat 2.86 grams
Saturated Fat 0.699 gram

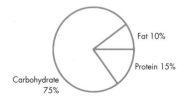

Fat 10%
Protein 15%
Carbohydrate 75%

Corn Cakes

Very New Englandy, these corn cakes served with warmed maple syrup. Can't you just feel it?

Doubling the batch is a good idea on this recipe. Keep 'em in the freezer so you have instant breakfast, brunch, lunch, dinner, anytime.

Fab Ideas

Pull 'em out of the freezer, heat 'em up, and change the feel totally. Served with poached egg whites topped with salsa or cream sauce, you have a Mexican fiesta dream breakfast.

How about adding 4 slices cooked crumbled turkey bacon to the batter to make a breakfast cake.

Or fancy it up: add ½ lb. fresh crabmeat and a tablespoon of lemon juice to the batter for crabcakes. Serve that up to anyone for dinner with the Chunky Roasted Red Pepper Sauce (see page 250) and tell me I'm not the next Betty!

1 cup cream-style corn
1/2 cup frozen corn kernels
1 egg, beaten
2 egg whites, beaten
3/4 cup flour
1 tsp baking powder
1 tsp Spike seasoning
2 tbsp chopped parsley
2 tbsp minced green onion
1/2 tsp pepper
   Nonstick spray

Place cream-style corn in a blender and blend until smooth. Add to remaining ingredients and mix well. Spray a nonstick skillet with nonstick cooking spray. Drop batter by spoonfuls onto pan and brown on both sides.

Nutritional:

Serving Size 3.5 ounces
Servings per Recipe 7
Calories 112
Total Fat 1.04 grams
Saturated Fat 0.275 gram

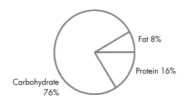

Fat 8%

Protein 16%

Carbohydrate 76%

Polenta

Cornmeal mush: usually full of cheese, butter, cream, and bacon. Consider all that changed.

Polenta now comes in this light version: fried in a nonstick pan and coated with Mushroom Sour Cream Sauce (see page 246). It's "new and improved" polenta.

Cornmeal at its best.

And not just a lunch or dinner dish . . .

Think Breakfast

Leave out the Nature's Seasonings, add crumbled turkey bacon, and pour warm maple syrup over it . . . love the sound of that for breakfast!!

1½ cups cornmeal
1 tsp Nature's Seasonings or salt
½ tsp pepper
   Oil
1 tbsp chopped Italian parsley

Combine cornmeal with 1½ cups water and seasonings. Gradually add mixture to 3 cups rapidly boiling water, stirring constantly, for about 3 minutes (it will be heavy and sticky). Turn heat to very low and cook 10 minutes more, stirring occasionally.

Pour into a loaf pan sprayed with nonstick spray. Chill thoroughly. Cut into ½-inch-thick slices. Fry in a nonstick pan sprayed lightly with oil, until browned on both sides. Serve with parsley sprinkled on top.

Nutritional:

Serving Size 2 ounces
Servings per Recipe 8
Calories 95
Total Fat 0.437 gram
Saturated Fat 0.06 gram

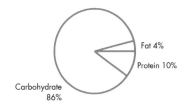

Fat 4%
Protein 10%
Carbohydrate 86%

Two of the best foods on the planet. Pasta, because there's so much you can do with it (as you're about to find out—and as you found out in "Entrees" and "Sauces, Dips, and Spreads"), and pizza, because what's better than pizza???

The pizza pie really needed my help.

What's the last food you think of when you think low fat?

Tell me the choice hasn't been flat stomach or a slice of pizza over and over again.

Never thought you could eat it, did ya?

Well it's with great pride that we at the Susan Powter Let's Eat America *kitchen bring you the Pasta and Pizza category in low-fat eating.*

Mangia! (That's All-American for Eat.)

Pasta and Pizza

Personal Size Pizza

You wanna feel like the worst mother in the world? Suzi (if you read *Food*, you know her; if not, I need to introduce you to her) is my book researcher and fellow mom.

Suzi's gonna make you feel like dirt. While researching "your very own little pizza dish," she not only checked all the facts and figures, confirmed the delicious taste of each and every single pizza dish, and repatriated the pizza, she had a little party (not feeling so bad yet, are you?). A bunch of friends of one of her daughters came over, and she turned her house into a pizza parlor. Each guest made his or her own creation.

As in make your own.

As in encourage creativity.

As in be a great mom with great ideas that boost growth and independence—the very spirit of the American West, the basis and foundation of this book, growth and independence. What do you think the Fourth of July is all about? INDEPENDENCE AND PIZZA, the two go hand in hand!!!

Suzi's How to Have a Make Your Own Pizza Party with Very Little Prep and Mess

Cut up onions, bell peppers, mushrooms, zucchini, tomatoes, anchovies, scallions—anything you want.

Get wild with pineapples and other ingredients.

Put all your condiments in bowls center stage and go to town making whatever you want.

You wanna know what the creative geniuses at Suzi's house did? Emily took leftover meatloaf from this book (love you, Emily—combining recipes from this book; get that kid a well-paying job in the organization) and made a topping. Sheila shredded low-fat cheese and had the cheesiest in the group. A couple of kids went wild with olives, jalapeños, and baby corn—now there's a combo—and everybody had a great time.

What a great idea—something I swore my kids and I

would do just so I could prove to myself that I was a creative mom. The book is almost finished and no pizza party yet. It's little things like this that can really trash your mothering self-esteem!

4 tbsp nonfat tomato sauce
1 burrito-size nonfat flour tortilla
3 mushrooms, thinly sliced
½ onion, thinly sliced
¼ bell pepper, sliced into thin strips
½ zucchini, grated
1 clove garlic, minced
½ tsp salt
½ tsp garlic powder
½ tsp onion powder
2 tbsp nonfat grated mozzarella cheese
1 tbsp grated reduced-fat Parmesan cheese

Preheat oven to 500 degrees.

Spread tomato sauce over tortilla. Top with vegetables in order given. Sprinkle with salt, garlic and onion powders, and cheeses. Place on cookie sheet and bake for 10 minutes, or until cheese melts.

Nutritional:

Serving Size 1 pizza (12 ounces)
Servings per Recipe 1
Calories 276
Total Fat 1.08 grams
Saturated Fat 0.093 gram

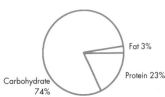

Fat 3%
Protein 23%
Carbohydrate 74%

Chewy Easy Pizza

"Easy" and "pizza" you're loving, right? But this "chewy" thing has got you stumped!!!

Understandably so, but let me suggest that as long as you're changing your lifestyle, why not change a few other things like—your idea of pizza.

Think chewy from now on.

Think quick.

Think easy, easy.

And think all the traditional flavors and Italian seasonings with any veggie and spice you love, love, love added.

Think pie.

(It's screaming pizza.)

Now add chewy, and you have your Chewy Easy Pizza.

 $\mathcal{W}$arning . . .

Make sure you check your dough.

Packaged doughs range from very, very low fat to unbelievably high fat.

FAT FORMULA ALERT . . . Do it.

Nonstick cooking spray
1 package refrigerated French bread dough
2 tsp Italian seasoning
$\frac{1}{3}$ cup tomato sauce
1 medium onion, thinly sliced
2 cloves garlic, minced
$\frac{1}{2}$ green bell pepper, cut into strips
$\frac{1}{4}$ lb mushrooms, sliced
2 medium tomatoes, thinly sliced
2 tbsp nonfat Parmesan cheese
1 cup shredded nonfat mozzarella cheese
$\frac{1}{4}$ cup basil
$\frac{1}{4}$ cup Italian parsley
Salt and pepper to taste

Preheat oven to 500 degrees.

Spray a pizza pan or cookie sheet with nonstick spray. Remove dough from package and unroll onto pan, pulling the dough evenly over the surface. Trim off excess dough.

Sprinkle dough with half of the Italian seasoning and the tomato sauce. Scatter the onion, garlic, pepper, and mushrooms over the dough. Lay the tomatoes over neatly. Sprinkle with Parmesan and mozzarella cheeses, the remaining Italian seasoning, basil, parsley, salt, and pepper.

Bake for 15–20 minutes.

Nutritional:

Serving Size $\frac{1}{4}$ pizza (9 ounces)
Servings per Recipe 4
Calories 232
Total Fat 3.26 grams
Saturated Fat 3.4 grams

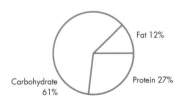

Fat 12%

Protein 27%

Carbohydrate
61%

Nonfat Vegetarian Lasagna

How American is lasagna? Totally, because America is the only place I've ever eaten it. Never had a good lasagna Down Under. (It's been about twenty years since I was there, but who's counting?)

Since we've improved the old version (makes me feel like I'm going to end up at the bottom of a river) by lowering the fat, we're going to claim it. And according to all our famous taste testers, this baby can be served to the best of the lasagna lovers and they'll love it.

Leftovers

As every lasagna lover knows:

Just as good, if not better, the next day . . .
Put it together with a green salad, garlic toast, and a little vinaigrette on the side, and you've got yourself a great-tasting meal.

Pssssst . . .

Don't tell anyone, but check it out: no meat. Chunks of veggie burger cooked and crumbled, loads of sautéed mushrooms, garlic, and nonfat cheeses. They'll never know, but believe me, your thighs will.

1 lb mushrooms, sliced
1 medium onion, chopped
½ cup chopped and sweated bell pepper
4 cloves garlic, chopped and sweated
4 vegetarian burger patties, browned in an oven or pan, and broken into pieces
4 cups marinara sauce
1 tbsp Italian seasoning
2 tbsp dried basil
1½ tbsp Mrs. Dash onion herb mix
1½ tbsp Mrs. Dash garlic herb mix
1 package lasagna noodles, cooked according to package directions
2 cups grated nonfat mozzarella cheese
2 cups nonfat cottage cheese
¼ cup nonfat or low-fat Parmesan cheese

Preheat oven to 375 degrees.

Sweat all the vegetables for 5 minutes. Add the browned broken-up vegetarian burger to the pan. Add marinara sauce, Italian seasoning, and spices. Cook over low heat for 10 minutes.

Put a thin layer of sauce on the bottom of a 10-by-13-inch baking pan. Follow with a layer of noodles and another layer of sauce. Sprinkle mozzarella cheese over and dot with tablespoonfuls of cottage cheese. Sprinkle with Parmesan and each of the spices. Repeat, ending with cheese on top.

Bake at 375 degrees for approximately 40 minutes, uncovered.

Nutritional:

Serving Size 9 ounces
Servings per Recipe 12
Calories 245
Total Fat 5.43 grams
Saturated Fat 0.8 gram

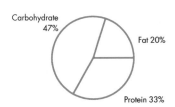

Carbohydrate 47%
Fat 20%
Protein 33%

Spaghetti Sauce

Here it is. The sauce you can serve to anyone who wants a full-of-flavor, down-home (in Little Italy) sauce to

cover pasta,

add to Nonfat Vegetarian Lasagna on page 234

or load onto Eggplant Parmigiana on page 164.

Food for Thought

If you're in the mood to cut way, way back on meat, all you gotta do is add more crumbled veggie burger instead of ground beef. You'll never taste the difference.

Olive oil spray
¾ **lb leanest ground beef**
2 **low- or nonfat vegetarian burgers**
1 **large onion, chopped**
4 **cloves garlic, minced**
1 **lb mushrooms, chopped**
1 **28-oz can crushed tomatoes**
1 **28-oz can chopped tomatoes**
1 **28-oz can tomato sauce**
1 **tbsp dried basil**
1 **tsp dried leaf oregano**
½ **tsp dried rosemary**
1 **tbsp fresh Italian parsley or 2 tbsp dried parsley**
1 **tbsp Nature's Seasonings**
1 **beef bouillon cube, dissolved in 1 cup water**

Spray large pot with olive oil and brown beef, draining fat off. Add vegetarian burgers, breaking them up as they cook. Remove meat/burger mixture. Add onions, garlic, and mushrooms and sweat until limp. Add remaining ingredients and meat/burger mixture. Simmer 45 minutes to 1 hour, adding water if sauce becomes too thick.

Nutritional:

Serving Size 13 ounces
Servings per Recipe 10
Calories 160
Total Fat 4.99 grams
Saturated Fat 1.83 grams

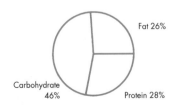

Fat 26%
Carbohydrate 46%
Protein 28%

Macaroni and Cheese

As American as . . .

Excuse me with this macaroni thing, but what the heck do you think Yankee Doodle stuck in his cap? "Stuck a feather in his cap and called it macaroni." Sure!

When you're talking about all-American, you're talking about mac and cheese. We had to find a way to lower the heck out of the fat because with all due respect to an American icon, we're talking killer when we talk about the "old" macaroni and cheese. So much fat, forget about it.

So here's what I'm giving you:

Mac and cheese that has very, very little fat.
Takes no time to make.
The kids go bonkers over it. (Bonkers?)
The best picnic, birthday party, barbecue, potluck, everything dish under the sun.

What more could you want?????

Butter-flavored margarine spray
3/4 **cup nonfat milk**
1 1/4 **cups nonfat cottage cheese**
1 **egg, beaten**
3/4 **cup nonfat sour cream**
3 **cups shredded nonfat cheddar cheese**
1/4 **cup very finely chopped onion**
4 **cups cooked elbow macaroni**
1/2 **tsp onion powder**
Salt and pepper to taste
1/2 **cup bread crumbs**
1/4 **tsp paprika**

Preheat oven to 350 degrees.

Spray a shallow 4-quart casserole dish with the margarine spray.

In a blender combine milk and cottage cheese. In a separate bowl combine egg, sour cream, cheddar cheese, and onion. Add blender mixture, macaroni, herb mixture, salt, and pepper.

Spoon into a casserole dish. Sprinkle with bread crumbs and paprika, and spray with margarine spray.

Bake, covered, for 20 minutes. Remove cover and bake 15 more minutes, until bread crumbs are browned.

Nutritional:

Serving Size 9 ounces
Servings per Recipe 6
Calories 307
Total Fat 1.93 grams
Saturated Fat 0.491 gram

Carbohydrate 56%
Fat 6%
Protein 38%

Macaroni Salad

Raise the flag, raise your hand to your heart, and sing the National Anthem because this is it. As American as it gets. There would be no pot luck without it. Churches would close (can't have a church picnic without Macaroni Salad) and family gatherings would dissolve . . . seems to me that the very fabric of our society wouldn't be the same without Macaroni Salad around. Thank God I've saved us all with this low-fat, nineties, great-tasting version . . . what do you think, am I in with the judge or what?

6 cups cooked elbow macaroni
½ cup nonfat mayonnaise
½ cup nonfat sour cream
2 tbsp rice vinegar
1½ tsp Nature's Seasonings
2 tbsp chopped parsley
1 cup defrosted frozen peas
¾ cup finely chopped nonfat cheddar cheese

Combine all ingredients well and refrigerate.

Nutritional:

Serving Size 7.8 ounces
Servings per Recipe 6
Calories 266
Total Fat 1.05 grams
Saturated Fat 0.153 gram

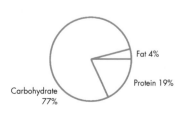

Fat 4%

Protein 19%

Carbohydrate
77%

Saucy, spicy, the flavor, the punch, the thing
that always stumps you. What can I put on it?
How do I make it taste good? It needs
something. . . .
   Something like:

> *Barbecue Sauce*
> *Eggplant Sauce*
> *Salsa*
> *Chunky Roasted Red Pepper Sauce*
> *Fresh Tomato Sauce*
> *Mushroom Onion Gravy*
> *Nonfat Sour Cream Cilantro Sauce*
> *Mushroom Sour Cream Sauce*
> *Etc.*

Dump it on, splash it around, sauce it up!

Sauces, Dips, and Spreads

▬▬▬▬▬▬▬▬▬▬▬▬▬▬▬▬▬▬▬▬▬▬▬▬

Eggplant Sauce or Dip

The best dip for veggies.

Great over pasta or rice.

An eggplant lover's dish.

If you're not into eggplant, don't even bother because this is eggplant through and through.

2 tsp olive oil
1 medium onion, chopped
1 large eggplant, peeled and cubed
4 small cloves garlic, minced
1 tsp Spike seasoning
  Juice of 1 lemon
$\frac{1}{2}$ cup vegetable broth
1 tbsp parsley
10 fresh basil leaves

In a large saucepan, over medium high heat, put olive oil and onion. Saute until just limp. Add eggplant and cook until soft and lightly browned. Add garlic and cook until garlic is soft, add Spike and lemon juice. Put in blender and pulse until smooth, adding only enough broth to blend. Add parsley and basil at last few seconds.

Nutritional:

Serving Size 6.7 ounces
Servings per Recipe 4
Calories 78
Total Fat 2.73 grams
Saturated Fat 0.372 gram

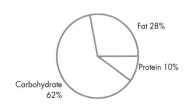

Fat 28%

Protein 10%

Carbohydrate 62%

Mushroom Sour Cream Sauce

If you have

An omelet to top . . .
Rice or pasta that is naked and needs a good covering . . .
A plain baked potato that is screaming for something . . .
Some Polenta (see page 226) that needs something saucy . . .

This is it.

Fresh mushrooms sautéed with onions, garlic, a little wine if you like, and fresh spices.
  Perfect.

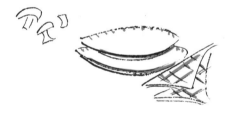

Nonstick cooking spray
1 medium onion, sliced thin and cut in half
1 large clove garlic, minced
8 oz mushrooms, sliced $\frac{1}{8}$ to $\frac{1}{4}''$ thick
$\frac{1}{4}$ cup vermouth or dry white wine
2$\frac{1}{2}$ cups vegetable or chicken broth
4 tbsp flour, browned
1 tsp Nature's Seasonings
2 tbsp parsley, chopped
1 tbsp lemon juice
2 tbsp sour cream (or more to taste)

In a 12-inch skillet sprayed with oil, sweat onion over high heat until limp. Add garlic and mushrooms. Cook until mushrooms lose their juices. Remove everything from pan. Add vermouth and 1 cup of broth to the skillet. Cook for 1 minute. Remove and pour liquid over mushroom/onion mixture. Put flour into pan and heat until light brown. Add remaining broth, seasonings, parsley, and lemon juice. Stir in the sour cream. Return mushroom mixture to pan and simmer for 5 minutes.

Nutritional:

Serving Size 6 ounces
Servings per Recipe 6
Calories 45
Total Fat 0.702 gram
Saturated Fat 0.097 gram

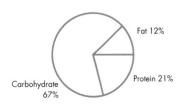

Fat 12%

Protein 21%

Carbohydrate 67%

Orange Cilantro Sauce

You look at the title and you think, absolutely not: orange and cilantro together has got to be foul, but I'm telling you it's delicious. You've got to be a cilantro fan, but if you are, this just may be your favorite sauce of all time. I needed the orange in this recipe because it was really gonna be a stretch to turn Cilantro Sauce into an American dish, but think orange and think Florida, done deal.

Dip all kinds of veggies in this, or spoon over chicken or fish—love, love, love it.

½ cup orange juice
2 tbsp lemon juice
2 tbsp cilantro
2 medium cloves garlic
2 tbsp light tamari or soy sauce
⅛ tsp sesame oil
1 tsp Spike seasoning
¼ cup finely chopped red bell pepper
2 green onions, finely chopped

Combine all ingredients in a blender except pepper and on-ions. Stir in pepper and onions. Let stand at least 1 hour.

Nutritional:

Serving Size 2 ounces/¼ cup
Servings per Recipe 4
Calories 22.5
Total Fat 0.250 gram
Saturated Fat 0.038 gram

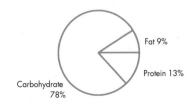

Fat 9%

Protein 13%

Carbohydrate
78%

Chunky Roasted
Red Pepper Sauce

This is it.

Our very own.

A new, low-fat, fab-tasting nineties sauce to pour over anything you want to pour it over.

Fresh red bell peppers, roasted and blended with garlic, lemon juice, fresh tomatoes, fresh basil, and spices.

An instant sauce straight out of a summer garden.

Sauce just for you, compliments of Susan Powter's Let's Eat in America, as an American, draped in an American flag, buying made-in-America products—how about it, your honor?

2 red peppers
2 garlic cloves
2 medium tomatoes, chopped
2 tbsp lemon juice
½ tsp Nature's Seasonings
1 tsp Mrs. Dash onion and herb mix
¼ cup fresh basil or 1 tbsp dried (fresh is truly superior in this case)
2 tbsp Italian parsley
2 tbsp vegetable broth, if necessary

Over hot coals or, in a broiler, cook peppers until the skin blisters and lifts. Place in a plastic bag for 10 minutes. The skins should come off easily. Put peppers and remaining ingredients in a blender and pulse until chunky smooth. Serve with fish, vegetables, pasta, chicken, or pork.

Nutritional:

Serving Size 3 ounces/¼ cup
Servings per Recipe 4
Calories 26
Total Fat 0.340 gram
Saturated Fat 0.043 gram

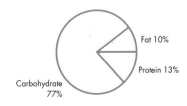

Fat 10%
Protein 13%
Carbohydrate 77%

Salsa

Put it on everything. You can't go wrong with
  fresh tomatoes
  jalapenos
  red onions
  bell peppers
  garlic
  lots of spices
  and lemon juice.

Can you get anything easier than this salsa? Throw all of the above in a blender, blend, and pour all over the place. Love salsa. Love this salsa. Dip any low-fat chip!

Please let me in . . . (subliminal suggestions to the immigration judge).

6–8 roma or medium tomatoes
  1 fresh jalapeno pepper, peeled, seeded, and chopped
  $^{1}/_{2}$ green bell pepper, coarsely chopped
  2 cloves garlic, minced
  $^{1}/_{2}$ tsp salt
  1 tsp Mrs. Dash garlic herb mix
  2 tbsp cilantro
  2 tbsp lemon juice
  $^{1}/_{2}$ cup red onion, finely chopped

Put three tomatoes, jalapeno, bell pepper, garlic, salt, Mrs. Dash, cilantro, and lemon juice into blender. Pulse until just blended. Hand chop remaining tomatoes and mix with blended ingredients. Add onion. Sprinkle with more cilantro if desired.

Nutritional:

Serving Size 2$^{1}/_{2}$ ounces/
  1$^{1}/_{4}$ cup
Servings per Recipe 16
Calories 19.3
Total Fat 0.233 gram
Saturated Fat 0.033 gram

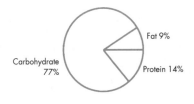

Fat 9%

Carbohydrate
77%

Protein 14%

Fresh Tomato Sauce

There's no gourmet, basil-y tomato sauce in my house, only real 100% American tomato sauce.

Hefty sauce to go over your angelhair pasta.

SAUCE to spoon over your grilled fish.

Or thick, great-tasting, hearty sauce just to eat from a spoon. Yep. Premenstrual, salty, tomato-y city right from the spoon.

Tomatoes from?

Italy? Do I see Italy anywhere in this recipe? Or are we talking U.S. tomatoes:

Beefsteak tomatoes from the east, like Pennsylvania . . .

Vine-ripened tomatoes from California . . .

Hanover tomatoes from Virginia . . .

I'm not sure it gets any easier than chopping up a bunch of fresh ingredients, mixing, and it's done. When I said "simple recipes" was I joking?

Suggestions from the Kitchen

Lumpy isn't good when you're talking mashed potatoes—we all know that. But lumpy and this sauce, don't ask how good it is . . .

Throw in some garbanzo beans to thicken and guarantee lumpy.

Fancy Schmancy

Get yourself a chunk of sourdough bread and toast it up.

Add a touch of your new lower-fat favorite tomato sauce.

Sprinkle on some low-fat Parmesan cheese.

And you've got yourself a low-fat Bruschetta.

12 ripe medium tomatoes, peeled (see below)
 3 cloves garlic, minced
 2 tbsp chopped Italian parsley
 2 tbsp chopped basil
 1 small red onion, very thinly sliced
 ½ tsp Nature's Seasonings
 ¼ tsp white pepper
 ¼ cup seasoned rice vinegar

To peel the tomatoes, drop the whole tomatoes into boiling water for 1 minute. Lift out gently and peel under running cold water.

Chop tomatoes. Add other ingredients and combine well.

Nutritional:

Serving Size 15 ounces
Servings per Recipe 4
Calories 101
Total Fat 1.3 grams
Saturated Fat 0.179 gram

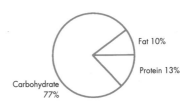

Fat 10%

Protein 13%

Carbohydrate 77%

Barbecue Sauce

Whip out the grill.

Tie the apron around your shrinking waist.

Get ready for some powerful barbecue flavor on whatever you like barbecue sauce on. We're talking bigger than mesquite. Beats the heck out of the average sauce. Flavors you'd never expect in a simple sauce. Check out the ingredients in this stuff:

Plum jam
Apricot pineapple jam
Five different kinds of seasonings
Fresh garlic

Oh yeah, oh yeah—you don't think these things are going to put out some flavor? This barbecue sauce has the

Rough face of Eastwood
Soul of Wayne
All-American quality of Roy

And is more Oakley than Annie (I had to end with a female cowboy, if you know what I mean)

This is *barbecue sauce!* Your chicken will never be the same. Grilled veggies won't be just grilled veggies ever again—and there's more . . .

Make extra because leftovers of this stuff go a long way.

- ¼ cup light molasses
- ¼ cup tamari or low-sodium soy sauce
- ½ cup chili sauce
- ½ cup ketchup
- ½ cup plum jam
- ½ cup apricot or apricot-pineapple preserves
- 1 cup finely chopped onions
- ¼ cup dried minced onions
- 6 cloves garlic, minced
- 1 tsp Nature's Seasoning (if unavailable, use ½ tsp each celery salt and pepper)
- 1 tbsp Mrs. Dash onion herb mix
- 1 tbsp Mrs. Dash garlic herb mix
- 1 tsp Spike seasoning

Combine all ingredients in a deep saucepan and simmer for 1 hour. If you want it hotter, add 1 teaspoon of dried red chili peppers.

Nutritional:

Serving Size 1 tbsp
Servings per Recipe 45
Calories 23.5
Total Fat 0.05 gram
Saturated Fat 0.009 gram

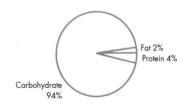

Fat 2%
Protein 4%

Carbohydrate
94%

Basic Cream Sauce

White sauce—who can get along without it? In the past, white sauce had the worst reputation in town. Now, thanks to Susan Powter's Let's Eat America kitchen, all that has changed.

When you're looking for the perfect creamy white sauce for:

> A solid base for clam sauce
> Alfredo with nonfat cheese
> Creamed peas and onions

YOU'VE GOT IT RIGHT HERE.

And if you want more than Basic White Sauce ... all you've got to do is add some Dijon Mustard Sauce.

Cream Sauce with Dijon mustard added = a cream Mustard Sauce.

Cream Mustard Sauce

Perfect with:

> Grilled fish or chicken
> Steamed veggies
> Asparagus
> Broccoli
> Cauliflower
> As a dipping sauce for a hot ham sandwich

More???

Creamy Lemon Herb Sauce

Made with fresh garlic, parsley, green onions, and fresh lemon juice. Try this over the Stuffed Peppers on page 172. Or just let it pour over fresh steamed veggies.

WOW, what a sauce. . . .

3 tbsp flour, lightly browned
2 cups nonfat milk
½ tsp salt
⅛ tsp white pepper

Add milk to flour over medium heat, stirring with a wire whisk until creamy. Add salt and pepper to taste.

Nutritional:

Serving Size 1 ounce/2 tbsp
Servings per Recipe 18
Calories 14.3
Total Fat 0.062 gram
Saturated Fat 0.034 gram

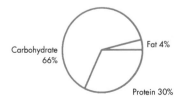

Carbohydrate 66%
Fat 4%
Protein 30%

Mustard Sauce

1 cup Basic Cream Sauce (see recipe on page 258)
1 tbsp Dijon mustard

Combine Basic Cream Sauce and mustard. Heat through.

Nutritional:

Serving Size 1 ounce/2 tbsp
Servings per Recipe 10
Calories 13.5
Total Fat 0.055 gram
Saturated Fat 0.031 gram

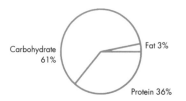

Carbohydrate 61%
Fat 3%
Protein 36%

Creamy Lemon Herb Sauce

1 cup Basic Cream Sauce (see page 258)
2 cloves garlic, chopped and sautéed
2 tbsp chopped parsley
2 tbsp chopped green onions
2 tbsp lemon juice

Combine all ingredients and heat through. If you want a little heat, add ½ teaspoon of dried red peppers.

(see page 258)

Nutritional:

Serving Size 1 ounce/2 tbsp
Servings per Recipe 10
Calories 14.3
Total Fat 0.076 gram
Saturated Fat 0.035 gram

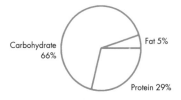

Carbohydrate 66%

Fat 5%

Protein 29%

261

Lemon Dijon Sauce

Combine five ingredients and heat up? *Come on America, This Is Easy* should be the title of this book. How about it: hollandaise sauce without the cream and the fat? Love it. Whatever you'd do with hollandaise sauce in the past at 18.5 grams of fat per serving, you can do leaner with this.

Pour over fresh steamed everything . . . .

Dip anything you want into it . . . .

And dump it all over your Eggs Florentine (see page 150).

2 tbsp Dijon mustard
⅓ cup nonfat mayonnaise
⅓ cup nonfat sour cream
½ tsp Spike seasoning
4 tbsp lemon juice

Combine all ingredients in a pan and heat just to a boil. Remove from heat and serve.

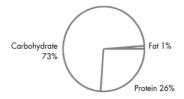

Nutritional:

Serving Size 1 ounce/2 tbsp
Servings per Recipe 8
Calories 19
Total Fat 0.0265 gram
Saturated Fat 0.00425 gram

Carbohydrate 73%
Fat 1%
Protein 26%

Nonfat Sour Cream Cilantro Sauce

This is the sauce that tops off your Chili Cornbread Pie on page 116.

It takes a minute to make, but take the time and make extra because it's great for dipping tortilla chips.

It takes your egg white omelet to a place it's never been before. . . .

It does wonders for your potato. . . .

Make it a salad dressing by thinning with milk and adjusting the seasonings to your taste.

And it's perfect for all salads.

Make it, stick it in the fridge, and pull it out whenever you need a southwestern cilantro-y dip.

1 16-oz carton nonfat sour cream
Juice of 1 lemon
1/4 cup chopped cilantro
1/2 cup chopped green onions
Salt and pepper to taste

Combine all ingredients well and chill.

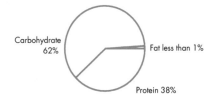

Alfredo/Carbonara Sauce

Too fancy for me even to pronounce, but good enough to eat, and eat, and eat . . .

This is a "dramatic reaction" dish. People will be floored (as our brilliant taste-testing women were) by this low-fat, rich, rich, fabulous-tasting dish. Perfect over pasta, baked potatoes, toast, biscuits, steamed veggies—just over, over everything.

So if it's a little drama you need in your life . . .

2 medium cloves garlic
   Nonstick spray
1 cup chicken gravy
½ cup nonfat sour cream
¼ cup nonfat cottage cheese
¼ cup vegetable or chicken broth
¼ cup nonfat Parmesan cheese
2 tbsp chopped fresh basil leaves or 1 tsp dried basil
1 tbsp finely chopped parsley

Sauté garlic for 3–5 minutes in a nonstick pan sprayed with nonstick cooking spray. Combine with remaining ingredients in a blender and process until smooth.

For Carbonara sauce, add 4 turkey bacon slices, cooked and crumbled, or ¼ cup nonfat or low-fat ham, browned and cut into strips ¼ inch wide and 2 inches long.

Nutritional: Alfredo Sauce

Serving Size 5 ounces/½ cup
Servings per Recipe 4
Calories 78
Total Fat 0.142 gram
Saturated Fat 0.014 gram

Fat 2%
Carbohydrate 53%
Protein 45%

Nutritional: Carbonara Sauce

Serving Size 5½ ounces/½ cup
Servings per Recipe 4
Calories 122
Total Fat 2.13 grams
Saturated Fat 0.679 gram

Fat 16%
Carbohydrate 36%
Protein 48%

Clam Dip

Clam dip is the best stuff ever with anything that requires dipping, and your new clam dip is better than any clam dip you've ever tasted. . . .

Dump it all over your baked potato.

Pull out the low-fat chips and clam dip, and snack to your heart's content.

Spread this on a toasted bagel.

Clam dip on everything now that you've got this recipe!!!

1 16-oz carton nonfat sour cream
1 6½-oz can chopped clams, with liquid drained and reserved
3 tbsp dried minced onion
½ Knorr vegetable cube, dissolved in ¼ cup clam liquid
½ tsp Nature's Seasoning

Combine all ingredients, discarding excess clam liquid. Chill 1 hour or more.

Nutritional:

Serving Size ¼ cup
Servings per Recipe 8
Calories 75
Total Fat 0.476 gram
Saturated Fat 0.045 gram

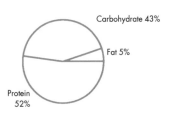

Carbohydrate 43%

Fat 5%

Protein 52%

Chicken Spread

Yuuuuuck. You're thinking spammy, mushy, who-knows-what's-in-it kind of stuff, aren't you?

Understandably so—because, quite frankly (frankly and beans, that is), that chickeny spreadable stuff has always looked and smelled a bit like dog food whenever I opened one of those little aluminum cans. We've gotta admit that it's never had the best reputation. But all that's about to change.

We are resurrecting chicken spread! When you eat this on a bagel with tomato, onions, lettuce, capers, and whatever other salty thing you want to put on top, you'll understand why.

Fancy Schmancy

Fancy Schmancy Chicken Spread? Is it possible???

Spread on French bread.
Sprinkle on low-fat Parmesan.
Stick under the broiler.

Or . . .

Stuff a tomato with it.

On crackers, it's the old chicken spread pâté to go along with your meatloaf pâté.

2 boneless, skinless chicken breasts
1½ cups chicken broth
1 clove garlic
1 green onion, chopped
2 tbsp parsley
½ cup nonfat cream cheese or Nonfat Yogurt Cream Cheese
(see page 280)
⅛ tsp white pepper
½ tsp celery salt
½ tsp Spike seasoning

Cook chicken breasts in broth on low heat for 15 minutes, or until cooked. Remove and place in a blender or food processor. (Reserve chicken broth for another use.) Add remaining ingredients and process until smooth. Chill.

Nutritional:

Serving Size 4 ounces
Servings per Recipe 6
Calories 69
Total Fat 1.04 grams
Saturated Fat 0.299 gram

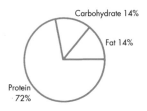

Carbohydrate 14%

Fat 14%

Protein 72%

Bacon Gravy

Can't be done. No one can make something with the name Bacon Gravy low fat and great tasting. Isn't that what you're thinking?

Well, naysayers of the high-fat world, make this recipe and tell me it can't be done!!!

Gravy over everything, that's my motto.

4 slices turkey bacon
2 green onions, minced
3 tbsp flour
1 cup chicken broth
1 cup nonfat evaporated milk
1 tbsp minced parsley (optional)
½ tsp pepper

Sauté bacon in a nonstick pan until crisp. Add onions at the last minute. Remove from pan. Chop bacon until minced and set aside.

Cook flour for 2 minutes in a pan. Add broth and milk and stir until thick and smooth. Return bacon and onions to pan. Add parsley, if using, and pepper. Serve with biscuits, over potatoes, or with eggs.

𝒩utritional:

Serving Size 3 ounces/¼ cup
Servings per Recipe 8
Calories 62.5
Total Fat 1.10 grams
Saturated Fat 0.379 gram

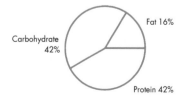

Fat 16%

Carbohydrate
42%

Protein 42%

Mushroom Onion Gravy

You can't have an all-American cookbook without a great gravy recipe. No can do, so we worked hard to get you the creamiest, mushroomiest, low-fat version of the gravy of your childhood and this one did it. . . .

What else would you put on your meatballs (other than tomato sauce)? Mushroom gravy.

Over mashed potatoes? Mushroom gravy.

Smothering your turkey? Mushroom gravy.

Meatloaf? Mushroom gravy.

What else would you put on top of anything that needed gravy?

It's gravy without the guilt. . . .

½ lb mushrooms, sliced
1 medium onion, sliced
1 clove garlic minced
1 tbsp minced dried onion
Nonstick cooking spray
¼ cup flour
3 cups vegetable or chicken broth
1 cup evaporated skim milk
1 tsp Nature's Seasonings

Sauté mushrooms, onion, and garlic until the mushrooms give up their juices and are limp. Remove from pan and set aside. Spray a pan lightly with nonstick cooking spray and brown the flour. Add broth and stir with whisk until thick and smooth. Add evaporated skim milk. Add mushroom mixture and seasoning. Reduce to 3 cups over medium-high heat.

Nutritional:

Serving Size 6.2 ounces/1¾ cup
Servings per Recipe 6
Calories 59.2
Total Fat 1.28 grams
Saturated Fat 0.413 gram

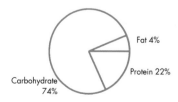

Fat 4%

Protein 22%

Carbohydrate 74%

Vegetable or Chicken Gravy

Warm.

Cozy.

Over everything.

That's what I think of when I hear the word gravy . . .

I just asked a friend of mine (male) what gravy means to him and he said, "Gravy is big, it's thumbs up." Very male wouldn't you say? But a good point—gravy is thumbs up and this all-but-no-fat gravy is two thumbs up.

Nobody needs to tell you what to do with gravy, just do it and enjoy.

2 tbsp flour, browned
1 cup chicken or vegetable broth
½ tsp Nature's Seasonings
½ tsp Mrs. Dash onion and herb mix
½ Knorr chicken bouillon cube

Combine flour and broth over medium heat, and whisk until smooth. Add remaining ingredients and simmer for 10 minutes. This makes a thick, spicy gravy. Cut back on spices for a milder flavor.

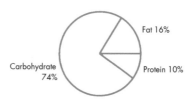

Nutritional:

Serving Size 2.3 ounces/¼ cup
Servings per Recipe 4
Calories 22.5
Total Fat 0.400 gram
Saturated Fat 0.034 gram

Fat 16%
Carbohydrate 74%
Protein 10%

Prune Apricot Butter

Prune Apricot Butter. I know you're thinking, "Gross, prune anything." But think about this: Whole food. Sweet, sweet, sweet. Works great with your body, if you know what I mean.

And this simple combination of orange juice, prunes, dried apricots, and a little honey is fabulous on toast, spread on your favorite muffins, in a fruit smoothie, or on top of grilled meat. Use it like you'd use a great barbecue sauce. Diversified, simple, and fabulous tasting.

1 cup pitted dry prunes
1 cup dried apricots
1 cup orange juice
1½ tbsp honey
¼ tsp ground cinnamon

Soak prunes and apricots in orange juice for 45 minutes. Place in a blender with honey and cinnamon. Blend until smooth. There will be little prune bits showing.

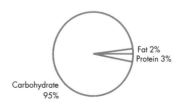

Nutritional:

Serving Size 1 ounce/2 tbsp
Servings per Recipe 20
Calories 65
Total Fat 0.133 gram
Saturated Fat 0 .012 gram

Fat 2%
Protein 3%

Carbohydrate
95%

Nonfat Yogurt Cream Cheese

Sounds gross, doesn't it?

Well, so does cream cheese, but we eat it all the time. And you can easily consider this a special version of cream cheese.

Make a batch of Nonfat Yogurt Cream Cheese once a week and store it in your refrigerator in your very American Tupperware (or any old container) with a tight-fitting lid and use it, use it just the way you'd use cream cheese—ON EVERYTHING.

Word to the Wise

Check your yogurt labels carefully. No fillers like tapioca, guar gum, or any other gummy thing because this doesn't work with that stuff. . . . We're talking pure yogurt or nothing for our American cream cheese.

2 cups nonfat yogurt (without tapioca or gelatin added)
¹/₂ tsp salt

Put any coffee filter in the bottom of a colander placed over a bowl. Put yogurt in the filter and let stand at room temperature overnight. Discard the liquid in the bowl. Add salt to the cheese and store, covered, in the refrigerator. Use just like cream cheese.

Nutritional:

Serving Size 1 ounce
Servings per Recipe
 approximately 17
Calories 16.1
Total Fat 0.052 gram
Saturated Fat 0.033 gram

Carbohydrate 56%

Fat 3%

Protein 41%

*So you've got a sweet tooth, who doesn't?
Everyone who's ever been to a dentist and been
bribed with a lollipop after a "good visit" learns
to love lollies. Whenever you were a good little
girl or boy and rewarded with that cookie, your
brain and heart made a connection:*

> *Good/Sweet*
> *Tasty/Sweet*
> *Love/Sweet*
> *Comfort/Sweet*

*That doesn't mean you are doomed to a
high-fat, dessert-y, no-hope-in-ever-changing-
anything life! If you feel like a dessert, have one.
A lower-fat version of your favorite—after you've
eaten a high-volume, low-fat meal: Breakfast,
Lunch, Dinner.*

*Not a thing wrong with something sweet and
tasty, but remember, the higher the fuel quality,
the better the performance.*

Desserts

Apple Brown Betty

You wanna know how good this is?

This looks and tastes like pie filling but isn't. Strong, sugary, thick . . . YUUUMMM.

If it's a filling, sweet dessert you're hankering for, whip up some Apple Brown Betty and go to town. Serve it with Vanilla Custard Sauce (see page 334) or ice cream and Caramel Sauce (see page 336).

American? Apple and Betty in the same sentence—how much more American could that be?

Thoughts About Betty

Great side dish with holiday turkey or chicken.

Vegetarian meal? Have a baked sweet potato, your favorite veggies, and Apple Brown Betty on the side.

And in the morning, it's an unbelievable topping for hot oatmeal . . .

1 1/2 cups bread crumbs—fresh or day old, not canned
1/4 cup reduced-fat margarine or canola oil
3 cups peeled and sliced apples
1/2 cup light brown sugar
1 1/2 tsp ground cinnamon
1/2 tsp allspice
1/4 tsp nutmeg
3/4 tsp salt
1 tsp grated lemon peel
2 tsp vanilla extract
1 cup raisins
2 tbsp lemon juice
6 tbsp apple juice concentrate, thawed

Preheat oven to 350 degrees.

Combine bread crumbs and margarine. Place half of the crumbs in the bottom of a baking dish.

Combine sugar, spices, lemon peel, and vanilla. Place half of the apples in the baking dish. Sprinkle with the sugar mixture. Add half of the raisins and half of the lemon juice and apple juice concentrate. Add remaining apples and other ingredients as before, finishing with crumbs.

Cover the baking dish and bake at 350 degrees for 35 minutes. Uncover and bake 20 minutes more at 400 degrees.

Nutritional:

Serving Size 5 ounces
Servings per Recipe 6
Calories 260
Total Fat 4.48 grams
Saturated Fat 0.804 gram

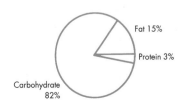

Fat 15%
Protein 3%
Carbohydrate 82%

Apple Berry Crisp

You don't even need to eat this dish . . . make up a batch just to make your house smell great. Apple deodorizer, that's how good this smells while you're making it.

This crisp apple-y dish with layers of apples and crumbs baked into a buttery, sweet casserole with almost no fat, served fresh out of the oven with Vanilla Custard Sauce (see page 334) or nonfat vanilla yogurt can't be beat.

Fab Idea

Here's a thought: serve it for breakfast and tell everyone that you've been up all night baking. . . . Sounds good to me. . . .

Serving Suggestions

Serve it with skim milk.
Add ¼ cup of low-fat granola.
Put a heaping spoonful on top of oatmeal.
For dessert . . . breakfast . . . a snack. Fabulous!!!

4 cups peeled, cored, sliced apples
1 tbsp cornstarch
1 cup unsweetened berry or apple juice
2 tsp Butter Buds
2 tbsp water
½ cup all-purpose flour
¼ cup quick-cooking oats
¼ cup brown sugar
1 tsp ground cinnamon
½ tsp salt

Preheat oven to 375 degrees.

Toss apples in cornstarch. Place in a 2-quart casserole or deep-dish pie pan. Pour juice over apples. Mix Butter Buds and water. Combine flour, oats, sugar, cinnamon, and salt. Moisten mixture with Butter Buds and water mixture just until crumbly. Scatter over apples.

Bake until crisp on top, about 45 minutes. If crumb mixture does not brown, place under broiler 3–5 minutes, watching carefully so it doesn't burn.

Nutritional:

Serving Size 5 ounces
Servings per Recipe 6
Calories 141
Total Fat 0.598 gram
Saturated Fat 0.1 gram

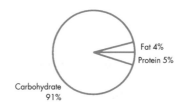

Fat 4%
Protein 5%
Carbohydrate 91%

Chewy Crust Apple Pie

I may be messing with holy stuff here, but I had to do a lower-fat version of the truly All-American dish of all time . . . apple pie.

The new and improved version of the American staple is a little on the chewy side. It's a nineties version. Think about a couple of dress sizes dropped, and I don't think you'll have a problem in the world falling in love with this Chewy Crust Apple Pie.

Crust

1½ cups unbleached or all-purpose flour
4 tbsp sugar
½ tsp salt
4 tbsp nonfat mayonnaise
½ tsp cinnamon
½ tsp nutmeg
1 egg white, beaten
3–4 tbsp apple juice concentrate, chilled
    Nonstick spray for pan

Combine all ingredients except apple juice. Mix until crumbly, adding apple juice just until it holds together in a ball. Refrigerate, wrapped in plastic wrap, 2 hours. Roll out to ⅛-inch thickness. Place in sprayed pie pan, trimming edges.

Filling

4 granny smith apples, peeled, cored, and sliced thin
¼ cup apple juice concentrate
1 tbsp Butter Buds

1 tsp cinnamon
½ tsp nutmeg
½ cup sugar
1 tsp vanilla
½ tsp salt
2 tbsp cornstarch
¼ cup nonfat evaporated milk

Preheat oven to 450 degrees.

Combine apples, juice, Butter Buds, cinnamon, nutmeg, and sugar in saucepan. Bring to a boil and simmer, covered, for 10 minutes (or combine in microwave-safe bowl and microwave on high for 5 minutes). Add remaining ingredients, combining well. Pour into prepared pie shell and bake in oven for 10 minutes. Reduce heat to 350 degrees and bake for an additional 45 minutes. For the last 20 minutes, put crumb mixture on top.

Crumb Mixture

½ cup chopped dates
½ cup brown sugar
1 cup fresh bread crumbs

Combine all ingredients in a blender and pulse until just blended.

Nutritional:

Serving Size 6 ounces/⅛ pie
Servings per Recipe 8
Calories 328
Total Fat 0.859 gram
Saturated Fat 0.238 gram

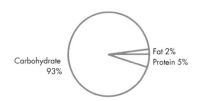

Carbohydrate 93%

Fat 2%
Protein 5%

Baked Apples

If you want the whole house to smell like you've been in the kitchen for days baking, make this.

It smells beautiful, looks unbelievable, and couldn't be better on a cold winter's night. It doesn't get more impressive when you need a holiday take-along show-off dish either.

 ssssst . . .

Warm this up and top it off with some Sour Cream Orange Sauce (see page 340).

¼ cup raisins
¼ cup coarsely chopped dried apricots
¼ cup chopped pitted prunes
½ tsp ground cinnamon
¼ tsp nutmeg
2 tbsp orange juice
¼ cup maple syrup or honey
½ tsp grated orange peel
4 large apples, cored without penetrating apple bottoms, leaving
  a shell ½–¾ inch thick
1 cup hot apple juice

Preheat oven to 425 degrees.

Mix together raisins, apricots, prunes, spices, orange juice, syrup, and orange peel. Fill apple cavities with mixture. Place apples in shallow baking dish. Pour boiling apple juice around apples and bake at 425 degrees for 30 minutes, or until apples are cooked through.

Nutritional:

Serving Size 12 ounces/1 apple
Servings per Recipe 4
Calories 274
Total Fat 1.06 grams
Saturated Fat 0.196 gram

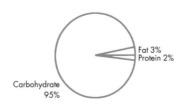

Fat 3%
Protein 2%

Carbohydrate
95%

Baked Apples and Bananas

This is the serve-over dish of the century. Serve over

Oatmeal
Frozen vanilla yogurt
Whole grain toast
French toast
Waffles

Or just eat it alone. How can you go wrong with Baked Apples and Bananas!

2 apples, peeled, cored, and thinly sliced
2 bananas, split lengthwise and cut in half
   Juice of ½ lemon
½ cup dark brown sugar
¼ cup light brown sugar
1 cup apple juice
½ tsp ground cinnamon
1 tsp vanilla extract

Preheat oven to 450 degrees.

Combine apples and bananas and put into a shallow baking dish. Sprinkle with lemon juice.

Combine remaining ingredients except vanilla in a saucepan and boil until sugar is dissolved. Remove from heat, add vanilla, and pour over bananas and apples.

Bake in 450-degree oven for 20 minutes, or until juices are bubbling.

Nutritional:

Serving Size 7.5 ounces
Servings per Recipe 4
Calories 228
Total Fat 0.56 gram
Saturated Fat 0.153 gram

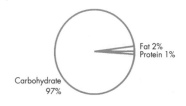

Fat 2%
Protein 1%

Carbohydrate
97%

Cherry Peach Cobbler

Talk about a lifesaver on a rainy day with the kids! This is yours. I'm telling you, this takes nothing to make. It's a throw-together project that will make you feel like the most creative mom on the block.

Top it off with low-fat ice cream or yogurt, and it's a done deal.

We're talking . . .

Sweet
Fresh
Easy

Four stars with the tasting moms and me, and low fat and entertaining for the kids. What could be better?

¾ lb pitted cherries or one 12-oz bag frozen cherries
2 peaches, peeled and sliced
2 tbsp lemon juice
¾ tsp ground cinnamon
2 tbsp quick-cooking tapioca
1 tsp vanilla extract
¾ cup sugar

Mix ingredients together and place in a nonstick 8-inch-square pan. Prepare crust (see recipe below).

Crust

1¾ cups all-purpose unbleached flour
1½ tsp baking powder
¾ tsp salt
2 tbsp sugar
2 tbsp reduced-fat margarine
⅔ cup nonfat milk

Preheat oven to 425 degrees.

Stir dry ingredients together. Add margarine and mix until it is crumbled. Stir in milk until the mixture forms a ball. Knead 6 times. Roll out to a thickness of ½ inch. Using a biscuit cutter, cut dough into 8 biscuits.

Place biscuits over filling and bake about 35 minutes, until golden.

Nutritional:

Serving Size 5 ounces
Servings per Recipe 8
Calories 191
Total Fat 1.9 grams
Saturated Fat 0.342 gram

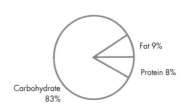

Fat 9%

Protein 8%

Carbohydrate
83%

ℒemon Cheesecake

Four stars on this *low-fat* cheesecake. They said it couldn't be done. Lindy's (of New York City cheesecake fame) would be proud of this cheesy, creamy filling with a golden crust.

There's no need to suggest anything when it comes to eating cheesecake.

My favorite way to eat cheesecake?

Slowly

Right from the fridge

When I'm really angry or frustrated

Or

You can top it off with your favorite fruits: apricots, raspberries, blueberries . . . YUUUMMMM.

And without a doubt you've got to try this four-star, low-fat, cheesy cheesecake with a puddle of the Black Chocolate Sauce (on page 346) or the Caramel Sauce (on page 336).

Crust

Nonstick spray
¼ cup graham cracker crumbs
2 tbsp sugar

1 cup sugar
2 8-oz packages nonfat Philadelphia-brand cream cheese
1 8-oz package low-fat cream cheese
1 egg
4 egg whites
2 tbsp lemon juice
1 tsp grated lemon rind
1 tsp vanilla extract

Spray pie pan with nonstick spray. To make crust, combine sugar and crumbs. Shake into pie pan, lightly covering sides and leaving a thick layer of crumbs evenly on the bottom.

To make filling, preheat oven to 350 degrees. Beat sugar and cream cheeses together until creamy. Beat in remaining ingredients. Pour into pie pan and bake for about 45 minutes, until set.

Nutritional:

Serving Size 4 ounces (⅛ pie)
Servings per Recipe 8
Calories 200
Total Fat 1.64 grams
Saturated Fat 0.682 gram

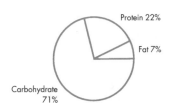

Protein 22%
Fat 7%
Carbohydrate 71%

Oatmeal Raisin Cookies

A dunker's dream.
Santa's new snack.
Curl up in bed with this one.
Dip these into your low-fat ice cream.
Sandwich low-fat yogurt in between two of these and lick the sides for days.

Sweet, crunchy Oatmeal Raisin Cookie.

COOKIE . . . Never heard the word until I came to this country. "May I have a biscuit [the Australian term], please," just doesn't have the same feel as COOKIE. . . .

What a great word, and this, my friends, is a great cookie.

½ cup oat bran
½ cup whole wheat flour
½ cup all-purpose unbleached flour
¼ tsp allspice
½ tsp ground cinnamon
1 tsp baking soda
1 tsp butter seasoning
1 cup brown sugar
½ tsp salt
3 cups rolled oats
1¼ cups raisins
¼ cup canola oil
2 tbsp nonfat yogurt
½ cup nonfat milk
3 egg whites
2 tsp vanilla extract

Preheat oven to 375 degrees.

Combine dry ingredients except oats and raisins. Mix in wet ingredients. Add oats and raisins. Drop by tablespoonful onto nonstick cookie sheet. Bake at 375 degrees for 15 minutes, or until golden. Remove cookies to a wire rack to cool.

Nutritional:

Serving Size ¾ ounce per cookie
Servings per Recipe 48
Calories 66.4
Total Fat 1.58 grams
Saturated Fat 0.165 gram

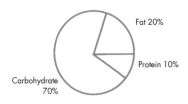

Fat 20%
Protein 10%
Carbohydrate 70%

Peach Crunch

The name of this recipe just about says it all. Straight from Georgia to your mouth.

You don't get much sweeter than this dish, and when you combine that with the crunchy top that comes out thicker than the average cobbler, you'll see why you don't need much else but this to satisfy even the sweetest sweet tooth.

*P*sssssst . . .

Do you want a big breakfast hit? Serve your peach cobbler in a bowl with some skimmed milk on top. What a way to start the day!

2 tbsp tapioca
¾ cup apple or cherry juice
1½ cups brown sugar
¾ cup flour
1 cup quick-cooking oatmeal
¼ tsp baking powder
¼ tsp salt
¼ tsp baking soda
½ tsp ground cinnamon
1 tbsp canola oil
2 tbsp apple juice
3 cups frozen or fresh peaches
1 tsp vanilla extract
1 tbsp Butter Buds or Molly McButter

Preheat oven to 350 degrees.

Combine tapioca and ¾ cup of juice. Let stand for 15 minutes.

Combine dry ingredients with canola oil and 2 tablespoons of juice.

Spread half of crumb mixture in the bottom of a 2-quart casserole.

Combine peaches, vanilla, and tapioca-juice mixture. Spread over top, sprinkle with Butter Buds, then spread remaining crumb mixture on top.

Bake for 30 minutes. Put under broiler to brown if necessary.

Nutritional:

Serving Size 6 ounces
Servings per Recipe 6
Calories 323
Total Fat 3.37 grams
Saturated Fat 0.353 gram

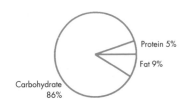

Protein 5%
Fat 9%
Carbohydrate 86%

Summer Peach Suzanne

Probably because I resemble a soft, sweet peach—wouldn't you say?

Or is it because I am a five-star rating? Because that's what this dish is. Five big ones from all of our taste-testing, recipe-making, hardest-to-please women.

You could serve this dessert at a wedding reception or to your best friend with coffee and get the same response: YUUUUUMMMMM.

It's simple to make, looks like a work of art, and couldn't be better. Isn't this the best cookbook you've ever owned?

6 ripe medium-size peaches
6 tbsp honey
1 tbsp vanilla extract
3 cups thawed frozen blackberries or boysenberries
2 tbsp orange juice concentrate, thawed
6 cups frozen nonfat vanilla yogurt

Place peaches in a large saucepan. Cover with water and add 4 tbsp honey, and vanilla. Bring to a boil, lower heat, cover pot, and cook for 5 minutes. Let stand for 5 minutes, then drain. Run cold water over them as you slip off the skins. Cut peaches in half, and discard pits.

Place defrosted berries in a blender with 2 tbsp honey and orange juice. Blend until smooth.

For each serving, place a cup of yogurt in a soup dish. Place a peach half on each side, partially covering yogurt. Pour ½ cup of sauce over.

Nutritional:

Serving Size 7 ounces
Servings per Recipe 12
Calories 178
Total Fat 0.359 gram
Saturated Fat 0.175 gram

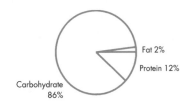

Fat 2%
Protein 12%
Carbohydrate 86%

Prune Apricot Whip

Good for the bowels and only two simple ingredients—the Prune Apricot Butter on page 278 and some egg whites. Fold together and bake and bingo, it's a souffle, light, airy, slightly tangy/sweet. A dessert that tastes best at room temperature. Serve this with Sour Cream Orange Sauce (page 340) and a spoonful of Prune Apricot Butter on top and you'll see what I mean.

Nonstick spray
1 cup Prune Apricot Butter (see page 350)
5 egg whites, beaten until stiff

Preheat oven to 350 degrees. Spray a loaf pan or 8-inch-square baking dish with nonstick spray. Fold the prune mixture into the egg whites. Pour into the pan. Fill a larger baking dish halfway with hot water and place the pan in the water. Cook in a 350-degree oven for 20–30 minutes, until the whip is set and slightly browned.

Nutritional:

Serving Size 2.8 ounces
Servings per Recipe 6
Calories 101
Total Fat 0.178 gram
Saturated Fat 0.016 gram

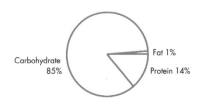

Carbohydrate 85%
Fat 1%
Protein 14%

Vanilla Pudding

Take my advice on this one: Serve it slightly warmed—with any dessert topping in this book:

Black Chocolate Sauce (see page 346)
Caramel Sauce (see page 336)
Blackberry Puree (see page 344)

Try it with the Baked Apples and Bananas (see page 292). Combine desserts—don't you love it!

1½ cups nonfat milk
½ cup evaporated skim milk
2 tbsp cornstarch
½ cup sugar
1 egg, beaten
4 egg whites, beaten
1½ tsp vanilla extract

Combine nonfat milk, skim milk, and cornstarch in a saucepan and stir until dissolved. Combine sugar, egg, and egg whites. Add to milk and cook over medium high heat, stirring until mixture comes to a boil. Turn heat to low and stir with a wire whisk until thick and creamy. Remove from heat and stir in vanilla. Cool. Cover with plastic wrap and refrigerate.

Nutritional:

Serving Size 7 ounces
Servings per Recipe 4
Calories 210
Total Fat 1.48 grams
Saturated Fat 0.534 gram

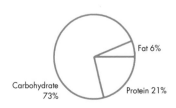

Fat 6%
Carbohydrate 73%
Protein 21%

No-Cook Citrus Pudding

No cooking?

As easy as it gets?

Tastes like pudding with lemon, lime, orange, and tangerine flavors?

Can easily turn into raspberry swirl (replace all the citrus with a 10-ounce bag of frozen raspberries)?

OH, what an afternoon snack.

What a great recipe!!!!

2 8-oz packages nonfat Philadelphia-brand cream cheese
1 14-oz can low-fat Eagle sweetened condensed milk
¼ cup lemon juice
2 tbsp fresh lime juice
¼ cup fresh orange or tangerine juice
2 tsp grated orange or tangerine rind
1 tsp vanilla extract

Beat cream cheese and milk on high speed until smooth. (A food processor is ideal.) Add juices, rind, and vanilla, and stir to blend. If mixture still has tiny lumps, pour into blender and blend until smooth. Pour into a bowl and chill.

Nutritional:

Serving Size 4½ ounces
Servings per Recipe 8
Calories 208
Total Fat 1.95 grams
Saturated Fat 1.28 grams

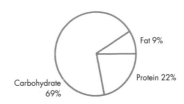

Fat 9%

Protein 22%

Carbohydrate 69%

Strawberry, Blueberry, Pear Mold

"Mold"—the only things appealing about the sound of this recipe are the fruits, but wait, wait, wait until you see and taste this summery, evening-on-the-patio dish.

Serve this with raspberry sauce anywhere, anytime, and it'll be a hit.

Pssssst . . .

First-time mold users need not be frightened! Every time one of our first-timers prepared this dish, it fell right out of the mold in one piece as if Betty Crocker herself were making it.

It's beautiful, elegant, and makes you look like a mold queen. What more could anyone want?

1 29-oz can pears in syrup, with juice drained and reserved
1¼ cups water
3 packets gelatin
¾ cup sugar
¾ cup nonfat cottage cheese
Nonstick cooking spray
1 cup frozen strawberries
1 cup frozen blueberries

Add enough water to pear juice to make 1½ cups of liquid. Sprinkle gelatin over top of juice-water mixture. Let sit 3 minutes. Boil 1¼ cups water. Add sugar and cook until sugar dissolves. Add to gelatin mixture, stirring well. Put pears, cottage cheese, and gelatin mixture in a blender and blend until smooth.

Spray a mold or a bundt pan with nonstick cooking spray. Place half of the frozen strawberries and blueberries in bottom of mold. Pour half of the pear puree over. Pour remaining berries over pear mixture. Pour remaining pear mixture over berries.

Chill until firm, about 2 hours. Dip bottom of mold in hot water for a few seconds. Place plate over top and turn over, holding the plate firmly. Decorate with mint leaves and serve with raspberry sauce.

Nutritional:

Serving Size 5 ounces
Servings per Recipe 12
Calories 113
Total Fat 0.119 gram
Saturated Fat 0.018 gram

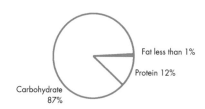

Fat less than 1%

Protein 12%

Carbohydrate 87%

Fruit Ambrosia Tapioca

Before you gag, hear me out.

First, the history: No one knows where tapioca comes from, and if they do, they won't admit it because knowing the history of tapioca screams, "I don't have a life," but everyone knows that tapioca has one hell of a bad reputation.

Frog's eyes?

Fisheye goo?

Just two of the nicknames that come to mind the minute I think of this lumpy, soggy, gooey stuff, but all that's changed since I started sucking up to the courts of this country to beg for citizenship and picked up a few great-tasting low-fat recipes along the way. . . . Tapioca has a whole new life, a totally different reputation. When you think of tapioca from now on, think of this fruity tapioca filled with pineapple bits, dates, fresh oranges, and coconut flavor.

Fab Ideas

A Parfait . . .

Layer, layer, layer with nonfat frozen vanilla yogurt, tapioca, nonfat frozen vanilla yogurt, tapioca, yogurt, tapioca, and on and on. . . .

How about a beautiful orange dip for graham crackers? (Tapioca's getting better all the time.)

Tapioca—a whole new life. If that won't get me in, what will???

1 cup sugar
1/8 tsp salt
1/2 cup quick-cooking tapioca
1 cup nonfat evaporated milk (see Note)
2 cups (or more) orange juice (see Note)
1 16-oz can pineapple chunks, drained and liquid reserved
   (see Note)
1 cup peeled and chopped orange sections
1/4 cup chopped dates
1 tsp coconut extract
3 tbsp flaked coconut
1 tsp grated orange peel

Combine sugar, salt, tapioca, milk, and juices in a saucepan. Let sit for 5 minutes. Bring mixture to a boil over medium-high heat, stirring constantly. Remove from heat. Let cool for 5 minutes. Add pineapple chunks, dates, and extract. Sprinkle with coconut and orange peel. Chill for 1–2 hours. Garnish with fresh mint leaves.

Note: The milk and juices should total 5 cups of liquid.

Nutritional:

Serving Size 5 ounces
Servings per Recipe 12
Calories 167
Total Fat 0.549 gram
Saturated Fat 0.384 gram

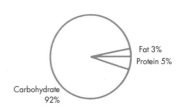

Fat 3%
Protein 5%
Carbohydrate 92%

Fruited Rice Pudding

I know, I know. Rice pudding: Gag me. But this is no ordinary rice pudding. Think about this: rice pudding baked with dates, raisins, apple juice, eggs, cinnamon, and nutmeg —you're looking at rice pudding like you've never tasted.

If you "take" your rice pudding hot, try spooning some nonfat frozen vanilla yogurt over the top, letting it melt to a cream—and see if I'm lying about how good this tastes.

This is the anytime dish.

First thing in the morning it's fabulous.

One thing you'd never really think about: it's a great "take-along" dish.

1 cup rice
2 cups water
1½ cups nonfat milk
1 cup nonfat evaporated milk
1 egg
2 egg whites
1 tbsp cornstarch
½ cup light brown sugar
⅛ tsp salt
1 tbsp apple juice concentrate
½ cup raisins
¼ cup chopped dates
1 tsp ground cinnamon
½ tsp nutmeg
    Nonstick cooking spray

Cook rice in water for about 15 minutes, covered, or until done.

Preheat oven to 350 degrees.

Combine milk and evaporated milk, egg, egg whites, cornstarch, sugar, and salt. Stir in rice, juice, raisins, dates, and spices. Turn into a baking dish sprayed with nonstick cooking spray. Place baking dish in a larger baking dish filled with 1 inch of hot water. Bake for about 1½ hours, or until creamy. Serve hot or cold.

Nutritional:

Serving Size 10 ounces
Servings per Recipe 6
Calories 304
Total Fat 1.42 grams
Saturated Fat 0.527 gram

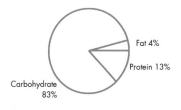

Fat 4%

Protein 13%

Carbohydrate
83%

Fruit Yogurt Shakes

Shakes as in plural. Five in one, to be exact. Monday through Friday? Check it out: You can have

Banana chocolate
Vanilla and fresh oranges
Pineapple, dates, and coconut
Chocolate yogurt with raspberries
Vanilla with peaches and cherries

Mix, match, and enjoy. . . .

BANANA CHOCOLATE SHAKE

2 cups frozen nonfat chocolate yogurt
1 medium ripe banana
¹/₂ tsp vanilla extract
   Enough skim milk to blend

Nutritional:

Serving Size 9 ounces
Servings per Recipe 2
Calories 262
Total Fat 1.835 grams
Saturated Fat 1.045 grams

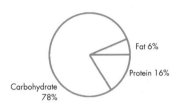

Fat 6%
Protein 16%
Carbohydrate 78%

ORANGE VANILLA SHAKE

2 cups frozen nonfat vanilla yogurt
1 orange, peeled and chopped
¹/₂ tsp vanilla extract
   Enough skim milk to blend

Nutritional:

Serving Size 9 ounces
Servings per Recipe 2
Calories 225
Total Fat 0.382 gram
Saturated Fat 0.210 gram

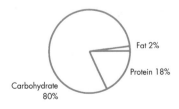

Fat 2%
Protein 18%
Carbohydrate 80%

Fruit Yogurt Shakes

TROPICAL SHAKE

2 cups frozen nonfat vanilla yogurt
¹/₂ cup fresh or canned pineapple
¹/₄ cup chopped dates
¹/₂ tsp coconut extract
    Enough skim milk to blend

Nutritional:

Serving Size 9 ounces
Servings per Recipe 2
Calories 274
Total Fat 0.57 gram
Saturated Fat 0.251 gram

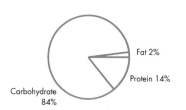

Fat 2%
Protein 14%
Carbohydrate 84%

CHOCOLATE RASPBERRY SHAKE

2 cups frozen nonfat chocolate yogurt
¹/₄ cup frozen raspberries
6 oz vanilla yogurt
    Enough skim milk to blend

Nutritional:

Serving Size 10¹/₂ ounces
Servings per Recipe 2
Calories 294
Total Fat 1.78 grams
Saturated Fat 1.03 grams

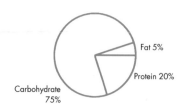

Fat 5%
Protein 20%
Carbohydrate 75%

SUMMERTIME SHAKE

2 cups frozen nonfat vanilla yogurt
¼ cup fresh or frozen peaches
¼ cup frozen cherries
½ tsp vanilla extract
   Enough skim milk to blend

For each recipe place all ingredients in a blender and process
until smooth.

Nutritional:

Serving Size 8½ ounces
Servings per Recipe 2
Calories 212
Total Fat 0.408 gram
Saturated Fat 0.217 gram

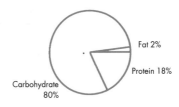

Fat 2%

Protein 18%

Carbohydrate
80%

Chocolate Orange Cake

I've got one thing to say about this cake:

LOOK AT THESE INGREDIENTS!

What could be better than this?

Pile it high with your favorite sorbet flavors or Black Chocolate Sauce (see page 346) and go to town on this elegant, great-tasting, fresh-squeezed cake.

Nonstick spray
1 egg
½ cup low-fat buttermilk
2 tsp very ripe bananas
2 tbsp fresh orange juice
1 tsp orange peel, finely grated
1 tsp vanilla
¾ cup sugar
1 cup self-rising flour
1 tsp baking soda
½ cup tiny semisweet chocolate morsels
Cocoa powder and orange peel for garnish

Preheat oven to 350 degrees.

Coat a bundt pan or 8-by-8-inch pan with nonstick spray.

In a bowl, beat egg for 2–3 minutes at medium speed. Add sugar gradually until mixture is pale yellow and thick. Add remaining ingredients except garnish and mix gently.

Pour into bundt pan and bake for about 30 minutes, or until a toothpick inserted in the center comes out clean.

Cool completely, turn out onto a plate, and sprinkle with cocoa powder and orange peel.

Nutritional:

Serving Size 1 slice (3 ounces)
Servings per Recipe 10
Calories 182
Total Fat 3.51 grams
Saturated Fat 1.84 grams

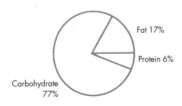

Fat 17%

Protein 6%

Carbohydrate 77%

Chocolate Bread Pudding

This is reallllly good, and we wouldn't have it if it weren't for the women of the heartland, those early settler women who taught us all never to waste a thing.

Some less imaginative cookbook historians will try to tell you that bread pudding originated in England, but close your ears to that kind of crap because when you think of anyone making anything out of something like a piece of bread—and especially chocolate bread pudding—you're talking HEART-LAND WOMEN.

This thing comes out of your stone hearth oven with a crusty top and tasting so good you will be floored.

Top it off with Orange Custard Sauce (see page 332) or a scoop of nonfat vanilla frozen yogurt.

$\mathcal{P}$ssssst . . .

Make extra because this tastes just as good the next day.

Ha! Bread pudding from England. Have you ever?????

Nonstick spray
¾ cup unsweetened cocoa powder plus additional for dusting
1¾ cups sugar
  3 cups nonfat milk
  1 lb day-old bread with crusts removed, torn into pieces
  1 tbsp vanilla extract
  1 egg
  2 egg whites
  1 tsp ground cinnamon
 ½ tsp salt
  1 tsp finely grated orange peel

Preheat oven to 375 degrees. Spray a loaf pan with nonstick spray and dust with cocoa powder.

Combine cocoa and ¾ cup sugar with milk in a saucepan. Cook over medium-low heat until dissolved. Cool. Pour over bread and soak until bread absorbs mixture.

Combine vanilla, egg, and egg whites, cinnamon, remaining sugar, salt, and orange peel. Place one layer of bread in loaf pan. Pour a little of the egg mixture over. Continue placing bread and egg mixture in loaf pan until the pan is filled. Pour remaining egg mixture over the top and bake for 45 minutes to 1 hour, or until crusty on top, puffy, and set in the middle. Let cool slightly and serve warm or cold. Some liquid will settle in bottom of pan.

Nutritional:

Serving Size 4 ounces
Servings per Recipe 6–8
Calories 208
Total Fat 2 grams
Saturated Fat 0.88 gram

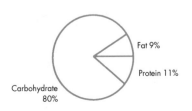

Fat 9%

Protein 11%

Carbohydrate 80%

Sticky Chocolate Cake with Pudding Sauce

Chocolate cake is good.

Chocolate cake is soothing.

Chocolate cake is here to stay in the nineties, thanks to this chocolate cake with pudding sauce.

Interested in something that's a cross between chocolate cake and a brownie?

Something that has little holes in the cake filled with fresh chocolate pudding?

Interested in a lower-fat version of one of your favorite desserts? I think so!!!

1¼ cups sugar
1¼ cups flour
½ cup unsweetened cocoa powder
½ tsp baking soda
¼ tsp salt
½ cup fat-free mayonnaise
½ tsp vinegar
½ cup prune juice
½ cup water
1 tsp vanilla extract
Nonstick spray
1 cup Black Chocolate Sauce (see recipe on page 346)

Preheat oven to 350 degrees.

Combine all dry ingredients and mix well. Add wet ingredients except Black Chocolate Sauce and mix thoroughly with an electric mixer.

Spray an 8-inch-square baking pan with nonstick spray. Pour batter into pan. Bake for 40–50 minutes, or until center springs back when touched lightly.

Remove from oven. Let sit 10 minutes. Poke holes in cake about 2 inches apart, and pour chocolate sauce over cake. Serve with a dollop of Chocolate Pudding (see page 326) on each slice.

𝒩utritional:

Serving Size 7 ounces
Servings per Recipe 8
Calories 344
Total Fat 1.88 grams
Saturated Fat 1.02 grams

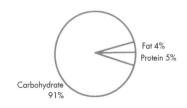

Fat 4%
Protein 5%
Carbohydrate 91%

Chocolate Pudding

TASTE TEST! TASTE TEST!

Have some friends over. Blindfold them. Put two bowls of chocolate pudding in front of them—one "from the store" high-fat regular pudding and then this chocolate pudding that takes minutes to whip up, is great warm or cooled, can be topped with any of your favorite pudding toppings, doubles brilliantly as an icing on your favorite cake—tell me if your friends can tell the difference between the chocolate pudding that puts fat all over your thighs and the new and improved, great-tasting, low-fat pudding of the future.

2 cups nonfat milk
³/₄ cup **Black Chocolate Sauce** (see page 346)
¹/₈ tsp salt
3 tbsp sugar
¹/₄ cup nonfat milk
3 tbsp plus 2 tsp cornstarch
1 tsp vanilla

In top of double boiler over boiling water, combine milk, chocolate sauce, salt, and sugar. Bring just to a boil. Reduce heat to medium.

Combine ¹/₄ cup milk and cornstarch, stirring till smooth.

With wire whisk stirring constantly, add cornstarch mixture to chocolate mixture; it will thicken very quickly. Reduce heat to low, cover, and cook another 10 minutes.

Remove from heat, add vanilla, and chill.

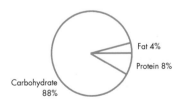

Chocolate Banana Cream Pie

Banana cream pie is one of America's—and my—favorites.

Until now, I didn't really believe that we could make an award winner (yes, I'm talking state fair quality) like this without the fat.

This little chocolate banana cream number got five stars from everyone who tasted, tested, ate and ate and ate this.

Make tons and don't expect any leftovers of this creamy, smooth, not too sweet but just sweet enough, low-fat version of one of America's favorite pies.

1 cup graham cracker crumbs
2 tbsp sugar
1 egg white, beaten until frothy
2 cups Chocolate Pudding (see page 326)
3 bananas, sliced

Preheat oven to 375 degrees.

Combine crumbs with sugar and egg whites. Moisten fingers and press mixture into pie pan sprayed with nonstick spray. Bake for 15 minutes. Cool. Place banana slices in pie shell, cover with chocolate pudding, chill, and serve.

Nutritional:

Serving Size 4 ounces/⅛ pie
Servings per Recipe 8
Calories 182
Total Fat 2.05 grams
Saturated Fat 0.656 gram

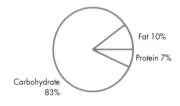

Fat 10%
Protein 7%
Carbohydrate 83%

Frozen Chocolate Cream

YUUUUUUUMMMMMMMMM!

Easy, easy, easy, melts in your mouth, and if it's chocolate you're dying for, add some Black Chocolate Sauce (see page 346) and top it off with fresh raspberries. Does it get much better than this?

This is the dish I think I should take over to the judge's house for an all-American food suck-up. You make it, taste it, and let me know if it's the one that'll get me in . . . .

1 can nonfat evaporated milk
³/₄ cup Black Chocolate Sauce (see page 346), chilled

Put beaters, bowl, and evaporated milk in freezer for 1 hour.
Beat milk until thick like whipped cream. Fold in chocolate
sauce until thoroughly mixed. Freeze about 1½ hours.

Nutritional:

Serving Size 3 ounces
Servings per Recipe 8
Calories 95.4
Total Fat 0.566 gram
Saturated Fat 0.336 gram

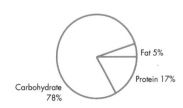

Fat 5%

Protein 17%

Carbohydrate
78%

Orange Custard Sauce

My grandmother, who passed away this year, is so connected to custard in my mind that it's breaking my heart to write this.

When I think of custard, I think

Thick
Warm
Rich
Grandma (rich as in texture, not rich as in Grandma was loaded because she wasn't)

Custard wasn't something I thought about until now, but with all due respect to Poppy (my grandmother's name; don't ask me why because for thirty-seven years I couldn't understand why my grandmother was named after a seed), this beats the heck out of what I always assumed couldn't be beat, Poppy's custard.

Ideas from the Chef

Serve it over

Angel food cake
Fresh fruit
Any chocolate anything

Warning: Double this recipe 'cause you'll eat half just cooking it.

1½ cups nonfat milk
¼ cup sugar
2 tbsp cornstarch
1 egg
1 tsp grated orange rind
1 tsp orange extract
½ tsp vanilla extract

Combine milk and cornstarch in a saucepan and dissolve completely. Add sugar, egg, and orange rind. Bring to a boil over medium heat and stir until thickened. Remove from heat and stir in extracts. Put plastic wrap over the custard to keep skin from forming.

Nutritional:

Serving Size 2 ounces/¼ cup
Servings per Recipe 8
Calories 60
Total Fat 0.709 gram
Saturated Fat 0.248 gram

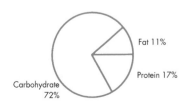

Fat 11%

Protein 17%

Carbohydrate 72%

Vanilla Custard Sauce

You wanna take a bowl of fruit and do something with it?

This all-around sauce (especially good when just cooked) can be thrown over any dessert in this book. Vanilla custard sauce dripping down your favorite dessert . . .

EXCUSE ME, what is better than that?

Cooled, this fabola sauce becomes a thick custard that is great, great, great sprinkled with cinnamon.

Comforting, soothing, custardy sauce/pudding . . . COUNT ME IN.

1½ cups nonfat milk
  1 tbsp cornstarch
  2 egg whites, beaten
  1 egg, beaten
  4 tbsp sugar
  1 tsp vanilla extract

Combine milk and cornstarch in a saucepan over low heat until cornstarch is dissolved. Add remaining ingredients except vanilla. Stir constantly over medium-low heat about 5 minutes, until thick. Remove from heat and add vanilla. Cover with plastic wrap to prevent skin from forming and refrigerate. Cool completely.

Nutritional:

Serving Size 3 ounces
Servings per Recipe 6
Calories 79
Total Fat 0.944 gram
Saturated Fat 0.33 gram

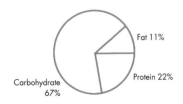

Caramel Sauce

Caramel apples?
Caramel candy?
Caramel Cracker Jack?
Who could live without caramel? All we had to do was take out the butter and keep the buttery flavor that caramel is known for—not a problem in the red, white, and blue kitchen of this bunch of gals.

Fab Ideas

Serve this

Warm, with nonfat vanilla ice cream
On puddings
On chocolate cake
Over apple pie (or forget the pie)
Warm or cold as a dip with freshly sliced apples

And enjoy.

1 12-oz can evaporated skim milk
1 ½ tbsp cornstarch
¼ cup light brown sugar
¼ cup dark brown sugar
1 tbsp reduced-fat margarine
1 ½ tsp vanilla extract
½ tsp butter flavor extract

Combine milk and cornstarch in a saucepan and stir until dissolved. Add light and dark brown sugars and margarine. Cook over medium-high heat until mixture thickens, stirring with a whisk. Remove from heat and stir in vanilla and butter flavoring.

Nutritional:

Serving Size ¼ cup/3 ounces
Servings per Recipe 6
Calories 109
Total Fat 1.03 grams
Saturated Fat 0.22 gram

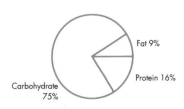

Fat 9%
Protein 16%
Carbohydrate 75%

Vanilla Yogurt Cheese Icing

A few minutes, five ingredients mixed together, and you have a low-fat icing that can be spread on top of anything!

Cupcakes or cakes are a given.

Spread this over cinnamon toast—instant cinnamon buns without all the fat.

Grab your favorite bran muffin—usually boring—and sweeten it up with Vanilla Yogurt Cheese Icing as a topping.

2 tbsp nonfat milk
1 cup Nonfat Yogurt Cream Cheese (see page 280)
2 cups powdered sugar
1 tsp vanilla extract
1 tsp grated lemon or orange rind

Combine milk and cheese. Gradually add sugar, vanilla, and rind. Add more sugar if you want a stiffer icing.

Nutritional:

Serving Size 1½ ounces/2 table-
    spoons
Servings per Recipe 12
Calories 78
Total Fat 0.056 gram
Saturated Fat 0.025 gram

Fat less than 1%
Protein 6%
Carbohydrate
94%

Sour Cream Orange Sauce

Yuuuuummmmm.

Pour this on chocolate cake. Dip any cookie under the sun in it. And when you serve it over Baked Apples (see page 290), get ready for an American dessert that is right up there with the big one—apple pie and ice cream. Blasphemous, you say? You'll change your mind once you try this little number.

1 cup nonfat sour cream
¼ cup honey
¼ cup orange juice
½ tsp grated orange rind

Combine all ingredients and chill. Serve over any fruit or chocolate cake.

Nutritional:

Serving Size ¼ cup
Servings per Recipe 4
Calories 107
Total Fat 0.043 gram
Saturated Fat 0.005 gram

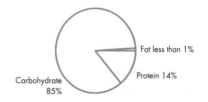

Fat less than 1%

Protein 14%

Carbohydrate 85%

Sour Cream Lemon Mint Sauce

Sounds a little gourmet-y to be in this book. I wasn't sure this was gonna make it in, but one bite of this over Lemon Cheesecake (see page 296) or over fresh fruit and you'll see why we turned our backs on the gourmets and put this in.

1 cup nonfat sour cream
¼ cup honey
¼ cup lemon juice
1 tbsp chopped mint

Combine all ingredients and chill. Serve over papaya.

Nutritional:

Serving Size ¼ cup
Servings per Recipe 4
Calories 104
Total Fat 0.052 gram
Saturated Fat 0.007 gram

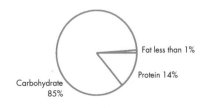

Fat less than 1%
Protein 14%
Carbohydrate 85%

Peach Vanilla Puree

Sure, you can pour this over fresh fruit, but don't even think about stopping there.

Think about this: Peach Vanilla Puree over nonfat ice cream.

Or—get ready, this will blow your mind—pour this little number all over your oatmeal in the morning.

Yuuuummmm. I told you these recipes were great!!!

1 cup frozen peaches
1 tbsp honey
$1/4$ cup apple or peach juice
$1/2$ tsp vanilla extract
$1/4$ tsp ground cinnamon

Combine all ingredients and chill. Add more honey if desired.

Nutritional:

Serving Size $1/4$ cup
Servings per Recipe 4
Calories 43.8
Total Fat 0.060 gram
Saturated Fat 0.008 gram

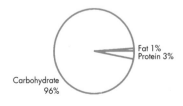

Fat 1%
Protein 3%
Carbohydrate
96%

Blackberry Puree

Blackberry Puree with your nonfat yogurt?

Blackberry Puree placed on your plate with fresh fruit on top! Fresh fruit takes on a whole new meaning . . . when it's swimming in Blackberry Puree.

1 cup frozen blackberries
1 tbsp honey
2 tbsp berry juice

Combine all ingredients and chill. Add more honey if desired.

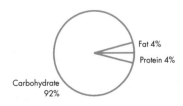

Black Chocolate Sauce

Enough said. The name alone is enough to ignite even the most tame sweet tooth.

This sauce screams

POUR ME OVER A SUNDAE.
Pour me over custard.
Pour me over ice cream, cake, bananas.
Pour me over anything—just pour me.

Fancy Schmancy

Easy, easy with Black Chocolate Sauce.

Simmer some fresh pears in their juice. Drain pears.

Put in a serving dish. Pour Vanilla Custard Sauce (see page 334) and Black Chocolate Sauce on top and serve to any chocolate sauce naysayer.

    1 cup water
1½ cups sugar
    1 cup unsweetened cocoa powder (Dutch process preferred)
    1 tbsp vanilla extract

Put water and sugar into a saucepan and bring to a boil. Cook for 5 minutes. Remove from heat and add cocoa, stirring constantly. Return to low heat and simmer for 5 minutes, until the cocoa is thoroughly dissolved. Remove from heat, stir in vanilla, and serve hot or cold.

Nutritional:

Serving Size ¼ cup/2 ounces
Servings per Recipe 12
Calories 116
Total Fat 0.94 gram
Saturated Fat 0.56 gram

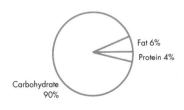

Fat 6%
Protein 4%
Carbohydrate 90%

Chocolate Raspberry Sauce

It's amazing what two simple ingredients like chocolate sauce and raspberries can do.

Dip
Spread
Fondue
Lick from fingers

Wherever your imagination takes you . . . when you're talking about Chocolate Raspberry Sauce.

1 cup Black Chocolate Sauce (see page 346)
1 cup frozen raspberries

Combine in a blender. Serve over cake or frozen yogurt.

Nutritional:

Serving Size 3 ounces
Servings per Recipe 8
Calories 174
Total Fat 1.28 grams
Saturated Fat 0.743 gram

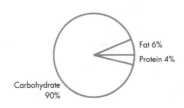

Fat 6%
Protein 4%
Carbohydrate 90%

Glossary

- Bouillon Cubes: use Knorr unless unavailable; use 2 regular size if substituting.
- Brown: cook over medium-to-high heat until item is browned on the outside.
- Cheese: nonfat Parmesan is available in both freshly grated and processed; nonfat Cheddar and mozzarella are widely available. The more well known the brand name, the better the flavor. Also, the sharper the cheddar, the better the flavor.
- Chicken, Vegetable and Beef Broth: use defatted; if unavailable, chill broth and skim off the fat.
- Chocolate Sauce: make double batches and store half in the freezer.
- Cooked Flour for Sauces: toast over medium heat until flour is a pale golden color. Cooked flour may be stored in a sealed container in the freezer and used as needed.
- Cooked Rice: cook a triple batch of rice. Put servings in amounts you use most often in zippered bags and freeze.
- Dairy Products: we use nonfat sour cream and nonfat cottage cheese in many of the recipes. The difference in name brands makes a noticeable difference in flavor. It's best to experiment with what is available in your area and stick to your favorite.
- Equipment: nonstick pots and pans make it infinitely easier to cook low-fat foods. They are readily available and getting cheaper by the day.
- Flour: use unbleached if possible; Wondra is the best for making gravy.
- Juices: use fresh fruits and vegetables whenever possible; the flavor is superior and does make a difference.
- Lemon Juice: may be frozen in ice trays and popped out as needed for recipes.
- Meats: check with your butcher, other markets, or health food stores in your area and see if pesticide-free and antibiotic-free meats are available. If they are not and you are interested in stocking your freezer with clean, untreated meat, call the National Organic Directory, a directory published by The Community Alliance with Family Farmers, and order one of their annual directories. They offer over 400 pages of resources for obtaining everything organic you could ever want. The number is 1-800-852-3832.
- Nonstick Sprays: we don't love them but they really cut down on the fat. Propellants are okay but you can make your own by filling a plastic spray bottle with canola oil. Watch out for saturated fats in some of the brands. Some health food stores do carry nonstick sprays without all the chemicals.
- Seasonings: use some seasoning blends because they add maximum flavor with minimum hassle, are readily available, and cut preparation time.
  The most common blends used in the book are:
  —Nature's Seasonings
  —Spike seasoning; comes in unsalted as well as salted
  —Mrs. Dash; all blends are good
  —Italian seasonings; any name brand will work
- Sweat: sauté without a measurable amount of oil; cook over high heat for a short period of time until the vegetables are cooked thoroughly but not browned.

Conclusion

Change your lifestyle. Don't you hate the expression "Change"?

As in give up what you love and change to something else. Change your lifestyle . . . to someone else's?

Let's get rid of it. . . . What the heck, we've bribed judges, sucked up like nobody's business, messed around with apple pie and ice cream . . . why not start messing with the English language? Call Webster and tell him to hold an opening, we've got a new expression.

We aren't going to change our lifestyles anymore.

What do you think of adapting the things you love just a bit so you don't die of heart disease?

How about cutting back just a bit on fat so you're not shlepping tons of fat wherever you walk?

Not killing ourselves and taking responsibility for the fact that eating tons and tons of fat has some side effects?

Heart disease

Obesity

Not so difficult to connect but so difficult to disconnect from our lives.

Let's adjust a few things so you can eat, enjoy, love your food, look good, feel better, and get on with your life.

• • •

There you have it. One of the most pathetic attempts at bribery you've probably ever read and a damn good cookbook about the foods you love with less fat.

Here's what I figured this book would be:

The best lower-in-fat recipes, respecting the tastes you love . . . done.

The answer to the much asked question, "What can I eat??? . . . done.

And as much fun reading it as it was writing it . . . you'll have to be the judge of that.

There are a lot more cookbooks to write because we still have to talk about:

What do we do with the kids?

How about those holidays?

We could even go as far—and I'm going to—as the best low-fat picnic in town.

Romantic and low fat—imagine how much fun we could have with that . . .

There's more to cover (with low-fat sauce of course) and I will, but for now:

    Eat.

    Enjoy.

    And be well.

    Susan Powter